NUGGETS OF FREEMASONRY

In The

GOLD RUSH DAYS

OF

CALIFORNIA

by

Granville Kimball Frisbie

It Is No Secret..... WHAT

MASONRY TEACHES:

MASONRY TEACHES love and kindness in
the home; honesty and fairness in business;
courtesy in social contacts; help for the weak and
unfortunate; resistance to wickedness; trust and
confidence in good men; forgiveness toward
the penitent; love toward one another; and,
above all, reverence for the Supreme Being,
based on a firm belief in the Fatherhood of God,
the Brotherhood of Man and the
Immortality of the Soul.

181936

Being some anecdotes of those early California Masonic pioneers whose *wisdom* and vision coupled
with their *strength* of purpose has helped produce the *beauty* that is California

FOREWORD

When Granville approached me last January and said he wanted to write something on Masonic History, I was not sure it would be successful, because many good histories have already been written. Then he explained to me that what he had in mind was a short history of short stories about mother lode Lodges, one that could be read by the average Mason in one evening or, at the most, two. This sounded logical and reasonable to yours truly, and I supported him.

Several times during his trips throughout the year 1968 he has come to me with chapters written from material he has collected. They all seem admirable to me, and I feel sure they will be well received by the craft because they appear to fulfill a need.

I have known this young man for many years; in fact, I have worked with him in the concordant bodies and have always found him to be a very likable person, a good Mason, sincere and devoted to his brethren.

Therefore, I feel sure you, too, will read what he has written with interest and profit.

Joe L. Shell, 33°, P.G.M.

PREFACE

It has seemed to me most fitting that an attempt be made to develop a short excursion into the gold rush days when Masonry and Masons came to California in sufficient strength to form Masonic Lodges.

Their advent became important to the forward march of civilization as they exercised their ingrained habits of charity toward their own, or indeed, toward anyone whose fortunes had fallen upon evil times in a wild and unsettled country.

In preparing to write a popular paperback larded with pictures, I was struck by the great paucity of pictures currently available in the more than sixty Masonic Organization's homes I knew were tucked away among the gold diggings, the mother lode towns, and the coastal cities, in which I have for more than forty years, lived. Hence this attempt to pique your interest, both Mason and non-Mason alike, with a brief recount of their beginnings and exploits.

Perhaps the very fact that your author is not a professional writer will add freshness. We hope it will. Perhaps the fact that he is also not a professional photographer will not unduly offend those more expert in the art. We hope it will not. The whole panorama of Masonry is not laid bare in this small volume. It is intended only to stimulate your interest to the point where you will look further. For example, in a Masonic Library you will find a four-volume history prepared by our late Grand Master Leon O. Whitsell for the Most Worshipful Grand Lodge of Free and Accepted Masons of the State of California, that will enchant the casual member to the core. For the non-Mason it may well develop such an insatiable curiosity that will lead to that fatal — for remaining such — question, "How do I go about becoming a Freemason?"

I wish now to express my grateful appreciation to all those who have made the book possible. Such a list is not as easy to compile as one would surmise. It includes my faithful and patient helpmeet, my wife, Elizabeth, whose expertise as a lifelong secretary is invaluable. It includes all those Masons who have found a way to allow me to examine records and books, paraphernalia and artifact, when keys and Lodge secretaries were out of town; bank presidents, and custodians, museum managers, and a great long list of devoted and hard-working Lodge secretaries.

The list is just about endless, and includes not only the Grand Secretary's indulgent ear, but the publisher himself, who also is a member of our craft. From one end of its production to the other, help of this nature has been forthcoming.

We sincerely hope that in its perusal you will find as much pleasure in its pages as we have in their preparation, as we journeyed up and down the State, and that you will recommend its reading to others that they, too, may enjoy it.

Granville K. Frisbie

CONTENTS

Here, the Flag of Mexico was changed for the Stars and Stripes. Here, the ebb and flow of history spawned the colorful web of fact and fiction. Around this historic Plaza seven stalwart Americans petitioned and obtained a Dispensation on August 1, 1851 to form a Masonic Lodge.

CHAPTER I

THE END OF ILL-REGULATED FORCE

SAN DIEGO LODGE NO. 35

John Judson Ames, six-feet-four and weighing eighteen stone, was, in the language of yesterday, a stem-winder.

What with Indian troubles and other troubles, the Americans at Old Town San Diego had their hands full. But not so full that John Judson Ames could not find time to serve on the City Council, publish the first San Diego newspaper, the San Diego Herald, with sufficient time left over to join eight other stalwarts and petition the Grand Lodge of Free and Accepted Masons of California to form a new Lodge at Old Town, to be called San Diego Lodge.

The year is 1851. It is April and the ranges are filled with cattle, the long stretches of Mission Valley are green with new growth, and the river is full and flowing fast with muddy swirls and eddys sweeping past the Presidio. A Presidio whose ruins are slowly crumbling on the tall hill, and as the river sweeps by the cluster of adobes at its foot, it etches its way across the flats and into the bay just south of two or three huts and hide-drying establishments, at a point that is called La Playa.

Since 1769, when the leather jacketed soldiers came with the Missionaries to colonize and build the Mission up the river at San Diego de Alcala and to establish a presidio or fort for protection and erect a Chapel for worship, the heights overlooking the village have looked down on what later became Old Town, we find that many changes have come upon the Spanish-Mexican scene.

The Missions eventually by the 1830's lost their power, the Indians and Mestizos have become unruly, surly, and demanding. The fact is that of a certainty these terrible, free-swinging, fast-shooting Gringo-Americans have just about ruined all that is left of the gentle Spanish culture so long grafted into this bit of Heaven-on-Earth.

But the Americans have come to stay. Their flag flies atop the pole in the plaza, and their soldiers, in this year of our Lord 1851, maintain the usual quiet that passes for peace in a sleepy-looking group of mud-adobe buildings huddled around the inevitable dusty plaza where every other door admits to a cantina. As the doughty historian of present day San Diego No. 35 Brother Orion Zink so aptly says, "The transition, while gradual, became more and more noticeable as frame buildings replaced 'casas de adobe' and intermarriages began to swallow up old Spanish family names."

The lurid towns of the far west had nothing on Old Town San Diego. Shootings were a daily occurrence and public whippings, a common punishment meted out to Indians, took place frequently on the northwest corner of Calhoun and Wallace Streets where an old upended cannon stood, used as a hitching post. While San Diego society was a grand mixture of cultures that in their expression ranged from feats of horsemanship to bull-fights where the bull was never killed but was brilliantly out-maneuvered. Then, at times there was the typical Spanish Judas-hanging of a stuffed effigy tied to a horse or bull chased through the streets terminating in capturing and suspending the effigy to the gallows. All this was over and against the swashbuckling bravado of the American explorer accustomed to survival because he was quickest on the draw where a plea of self-defense usually sufficed. Now there appeared a new breed of men bent on permanent settlement, and with them their families.

Into this picture came the early Freemasons. They, too, were Americans, arriving with the earliest ships as well as overland in the parties braving the westward march of the conestogas towards the gold fields. In this year of 1851 there was not only John Judson Ames, but James W. Robinson, an

This building on "H" Street (Market) near 6th was the home of San Diego Lodge No. 35 from 1882 until 1911 when it moved to more elegant quarters on Ash Street. Counting Old Town as a single home, the Lodge now occupies its sixth Temple.

Copy of an old print showing the Dunham Building (left) at 748 Fifth Street, San Diego. Courtesy of San Diego Lodge No. 35. F. & A.M. Into these quarters the Lodge moved on April 4, 1870 after a quick decision.

Ohioan who had been governor of the State of Texas, now the first Secretary of San Diego Lodge, and Agostin Haraszthy, a "Count" in his native Hungary, elected sheriff the year before, and John Cook, Assemblyman and first Junior Warden.

There was also Bro. Willliam C. Ferrell, the first Worshipful Master under the Dispensation, and Daniel Barbee, Major U.S. Army, R. E. Raymond, merchant, and William H. Moon, the first Tyler who endeavored to keep the brethren from interruption and whose post was outside, not inside the building, probably the Exchange Hotel, where he paced up and down beside the door, we assume with six-shooter at his side.

News travelled slowly, but by September 4, 1851 the Right Worshipful B. D. Hyam, Deputy Grand Master at Sacramento had returned to San Diego its Dispensation to form a Lodge. California Freemasonry can count itself "the essence of the true craftmanship" because it is the distilled result of many lines of jurisdictions and heritage combined into one unified and perfectly blended whole. The men who formed this first Lodge of Masons south of the Tehachapi Mountains came from many varied locations and with them came just as varied lines of Masonic ritual and thought.

However beneficial to the future of Masonry in California, the Lodge at San Diego had its growing pains. As I am sure his grandson today can testify, the first Master under the Charter, W. Bro. Philip Crosthwaite, took a firm grip upon the reins as the Lodge, like a skittish colt, took real handling to avoid wrecking the venture. George Hooper was the first to be accepted for membership but he was not the first to be accorded the Master's Degree. Many a slip-up was yet to come. Business was first conducted in the Apprentice degree, and along the side of the page of minutes, probably made later by a Grand Master reviewer, is seen the notation, "wrong." That pops up for many years on many occasions.

In fact, the Lodge once was called from labor to refreshment and business was again resumed a week later, so said the minutes, with the usual notation of "wrong" in the margin.

As Brother Zink, our careful historian, says, "It must have been the view of the great, peaceful blue ocean, the quiet waters of the bay and the salubrious climate that appealed to those road-weary travelers, for the San Diego that greeted them offered little in attraction" even in 1852 when the Dispensation was extended for another year because our zealous Deputy Grand Master Hyam had detected more places in the minutes he could insert the word "wrong." We suspect that there is more than meets the eye, for instance, such as certain brethren of San Diego Lodge being in favor of separating California into two States with San Diego the southern Capitol, and annexation to the list of slave States a foregone conclusion.

Every Mason knows that in June and December we celebrate our two patron Saints, St. John the Baptist and St. John the Evangelist. In the years of the early 1850's these patrons loomed more importantly than today in the eyes of the Fraternity. Take the one in Old Town about June 24, 1852 when our Lodge decided to hold a celebration. Let us quote from the *Herald*, of which John Judson Ames is the Editor, Owner, as well as typesetter who says, "San Diego Lodge, U.D., celebrated the nativity of St. John the Baptist, their Patron Saint, in a spirited and appropriate manner on the 24th; and as this was the first demonstration of the kind ever made in this region it attracted no little attention from the native population. . . . Although they were prohibited by the Padre from witnessing the ceremonies, many of them satisfied their curiosity by skulking around corners, and peeping out of windows and half closed doors. . . . When it is considered that there are so many towns along the six hundred miles of coast, between this point and San Francisco, some far exceeding this

{Casa de Bandini}
Built about 1846-7 for Gen. Kearny and used for years as the terminus of stage line and a hostelry.

The old Estudillo homestead known as "Ramona's Marriage Place" faces the Plaza where California began; the shaded smooth lawn in the photo on the right a far cry from the dusty Mexican Plaza of the early Californios.

This landmark, built in 1825 as the home of the Estudillo family, was made famous by Helen Hunt Jackson as part of the setting for her novel "Ramona." Perhaps no other spot in the old Spanish Village, where both San Diego and California itself began, has become more popular to our modern visitor. Like all proper homes it was built around a flower-filled patio and fountain, all rooms opening upon it from the interior, away from the noise, the dust, the flies and the horses of the street outside.

in point of population and that San Diego can boast of having erected the first and at present the only Lodge in Southern California, we think the brethren have reason to be proud of the fact, and of the occasion that called them together. . . . When it is remembered that San Diego Lodge commenced work with but seven members, all there were in the whole County, and that four of the original members are now absent, the fraternity may well be proud of the respectable number that turned out on this occasion."

Can we not imagine the dark eyed señoritas who had the courage to steal glances at the "heretics" through half closed lattices? Judson Ames thought so, and said so, in his chronicle of this event. And a few days later the resident Catholic Priest issued a formal Bull forbidding any of his flock to be present where the principal address was to be delivered, or even go into the street during the time the procession passed, on pain of being damned to all eternity. Had he forgotten that he himself headed a procession dressed in full regalia to lay a cornerstone of a new Roman Catholic Church a few months before? And that on this occasion much of the money contributed for the same came from the pockets of these same Protestants?

Time marches on. The "great city" of San Diego now consists of three elements, the "Playa" and "Old Town" and "New Town." Here at long last comes "old" Mr. John Phoenix himself, about as good as Mark Twain to a great many of his fans, and more formally known as Lt. George H. Derby, U.S. Army Engineers. But our Lt. Derby is actually barely in his twenties in a corporeal sense, but wise beyond his years in a spiritual sense.

The Lodge has entered its third year and still no Charter. Let us quote the key entry in the minutes, "Bro. Geo. A. Derby, Past Master of Sonoma (Temple) Lodge, being in-

The famous Scottish Rite Memorial Center in colorful Mission Valley.

vited by Br. Wm. C. Ferrell, W.M., presided at the meeting." It was Derby who turned the waters of the San Diego River into False Bay (Mission Bay). It was Derby who was elected a member of "this Lodge after a favorable report of the committee" and it was he who took the Lodge's life into his hands and went to San Francisco where the Committee on Dispensations and Charters had reported San Diego among those whom they had received "no returns." It was Derby who was appointed Grand Sword Bearer of this same Grand Lodge Convocation, and it was no less than this same astute young man who returned to San Diego with a Charter for a Lodge that had been nineteenth in order in point of age of its founding among the Lodges of the State, but found itself last to have a petition cleared and became No. 35 on the Grand Lodge Roster.

Derby was a man of real discernment. While his note in the minutes said in Latin: "magna est veritas et prevalabit"— great is Truth and it shall prevail — his delight in panning every manner of politician during his short tenure as editor of the Herald, substituting for Brother Ames while the old curmudgeon was out of town, has brought his delightful nonsense a permanent place in the annals of early California. Masonry, in San Diego, has had no greater champion.

Without attention to the many episodes of human foibles and weakness that marks these early heroic characters, stalwarts all, and members of the Masonic Fraternity, who composed the growing community as its most influential and calming influence, no narrative would be complete without its final anecdote of just how San Diego Lodge came to be removed from "Old Town" to a place called "New Town" that generally was known as Davis's and Horton's Folly.

As the newer part of San Diego grew, Masons arrived from other climes. Inevitably, it being four or more miles to go either by walking or riding a horse-drawn vehicle, or of course, horseback, the Masons of New Town got together and importuned the brethren at Old Town to assist them to obtain the formation of a new Lodge to be called "Monumental Lodge." The reaction was vigorous protest against it to their superiors at Grand Lodge. The year was 1870.

On the surface all was calm, but on April 4 Bro. E. B. Gifford made a motion to remove the Old Town Lodge to the Dunham Building, 748 5th Street in New Town. Motion carried sixteen to three because only three "Old Towners" had bothered to come to Lodge, the sixteen being all from the newer part of San Diego. So, without a moment of delay, the Lodge's property was loaded into a wagon and taken to its new quarters, that selfsame night.

The uproar over this surprise move, we leave to the reader to surmise. The Grand Master had previously suggested to the new group when they appeared before him with the matter of the formation of a new Lodge at San Diego in mind, that they first affiliate with No. 35 and in his subsequent report to Grand Lodge only said, "The brethren adopted this suggestion with surprising alacrity."

The year, I think we mentioned, was 1870. Begun in January and finished in September, with 96 sleeping rooms, a dining room, a bar and an office, was the Horton House, built by a man who now would be called a "35-er." (To those of you not "in the know" that is a "de-luxe" member of this "cushiest" of Lodges, one whose zeal and good deeds make San Diego 35 a Lodge to reckon with). Where this hotel once stood, now stands the U. S. Grant Hotel. By that year, San Diego had reached about 2,000 souls, and San Diego Lodge No. 35 just 52.

And from this number has sprung one of the finest Lodges of Masons in the State of California. May their tribe increase.

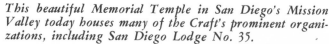

This beautiful Memorial Temple in San Diego's Mission Valley today houses many of the Craft's prominent organizations, including San Diego Lodge No. 35.

CHAPTER II

THE GEMS OF THE SOUTHERN MINES

CALAVERAS LODGE NO. 78
TUOLUMNE LODGE NO. 8
COLUMBIA LODGE NO. 28
BEAR MOUNTAIN LODGE NO. 76
YOSEMITE LODGE NO. 99
MOKELUMNE LODGE NO. 31
CAMPO SECO LODGE NO. 100
ORPHIR LODGE NO. 33

Many of these Lodges are inseparably intertwined. The first Masonic Lodge in Calaveras County, which County, just in passing, extends from the first grassy slopes of the big valley up, up the steep Sierras to Alpine County and Ebbetts Pass, was that of Mokelumne Hill, Chartered May 6, 1853. It burned out and received a duplicate Charter. It burned out again in 1879, struggled on, finally consolidating with Calaveras in 1883.

Campo Seco, the old mining town, received its "Century Charter" No. 100, May 8, 1856. Mining dwindled and the Lodge made a noble fight to maintain its existence. It was permitted to move to Valley Springs but never found suitable quarters, so in 1897 it too consolidated with Calaveras Lodge No. 78.

When you visit Washington, D.C. and inspect the Washington Mounment, be sure to look carefully for a certain block of stone, for that block of stone was the unit of granite purchased by Calaveras No. 78 on April 7, 1855 for the sum of $25.00 contributed by the Lodge.

Meeting first at Temperance Hall, in the town of San Andreas, now County seat of Calaveras County, Calaveras Lodge then moved to a building built by the Independent Order of Odd Fellows, owned jointly by them and us and used until 1900. Adjacent is the old Court House, where, on its second floor, the trial of Joaquin Murietta was held, and Benjamin Thorne, the sheriff in whose custody he remained, was a member of Calaveras Lodge No. 78.

The town of San Andreas was established by the Spanish and Mexican community, translating to our Saint Andrew. The present Lodge edifice, now at the corner of Main and St. Charles Streets, still houses the two fraternal groups, historically close throughout the passing years.

How many modern Master Masons have heard of the Grand Lodge Circular and the Lodge Black Book?

About the 1888 period, both before and after, Grand Lodge sent a quarterly circular to all its constituent Lodges revealing all those who had been rejected for the degrees, suspended for non-payment of dues, expelled, or reinstated after suspension for non-payment of dues.

Many Lodges were commonly confronted with elections that gave the dark aspect of as many as a half dozen or more negroid cubes mixed with the bright white spheres. Each Lodge maintained a bound ledger embossed by the manufacturer with the words "Black Book" on its cover. On its pages were the names, dates, and other pertinent data of those who still await without — with what patience we leave to the reader to determine.

These Black Books were a necessity of the times. Many men appeared at our portals voluntarily. Not all were found to measure up to the ancient requirements. With the play of events, the ebb and flow of tides of humanity in the ever evanescent search for precious metal, Masonry, too, evolved a way of life which suited her needs. She changes men, helps them to find themselves, to give their best; men seldom change her, and then, but slowly.

These old Lodge Books are only a ruse to present the over-one-hundred-year-old Ballot Box, carved entirely by jack-knife, brought round the horn on a sailing vessel, and used in La Grange Lodge No. 99, now Yosemite Lodge No. 99 at Merced.

For nearly fifty years Masonry has flourished in this modern structure in the friendly City of Merced, County Seat of Merced County.

Not a hanging! This is a real vivid cornerstone laying in 1917, one upon which the building was erected at 1810 "M" Street in Merced for Yosemite Lodge No. 99. Note the Brass Band, Grand Lodge Officials, the boy in the foreground in knee pants, and the piano in left background. (Copied from snapshot by author)

YOSEMITE LODGE NO. 99

While Masonry extended from the broad gates of Mexico at San Ysidro, to the Oregon border, and from the snow-capped Sierras to the Golden Gates, its early concentration centered about the foothills along the western slopes of the Sierras — long known to the world as the mother lode.

The southernmost gateway to the mother lode, proverbial as the southern mines, was the city of Merced, county capitol of Merced County, and while not the birthplace, it has become, since 1873, the home of one of our pioneer Lodges.

Yosemite Lodge began as La Grange Lodge No. 99 and was located in the adjacent county of Stanislaus in the mining town of La Grange on the road to Coulterville which long supported the craft.

Chartered May 8, 1856, La Grange Lodge No. 99 still flourishes in Merced as Yosemite Lodge No. 99 after its removal from La Grange, and consolidation with Yosemite Lodge. It has nurtured several Masonic "greats" on its rolls. One of the most colorful among them was Fred Becker.

Born in Baden, Germany, he came to the U.S.A. as a young man of nineteen and served in the Arkansas Cavalry in the Mexican War in the same regiment in which Bro. Albert Pike, 33°, was a Captain, his Colonel being killed in the hard-fought battle of Buena Vista in what is now the middle of downtown Mexico City.

Mustered out, he received his degrees in Arkansas, came to California and joined La Grange just two months after it received its Charter, served as Junior Deacon, Junior Warden, and as Master in 1867, 1868, 1869, and again in 1870 and 1871. His devoted and faithful attention to the good of the Lodge made him the favorite of his time.

Another brother of fame is Hiram N. Rucker. Born in Missouri, he came across the plains when he was eight years of age in the favorite jet transportation of his time — the ox team. Settling in Santa Clara where he received much of his schooling, he graduated as a doctor of medicine from the University of the Pacific sans scholarship, but with a mighty urge for hard work.

Locating in Merced, Bro. Rucker flourished handily both as a doctor and as a member of Yosemite Lodge, being raised just before the move from Stanislaus to Merced county. He was Master in 1877-78-79. For more years than a few he attended Grand Lodge annually, where he served as Senior Grand Deacon, then as Junior Grand Warden, advancing to Grand Master in 1887. As an orator, few were his equal, either then or now.

Yosemite Lodge No. 99 is located in one of the warmly responsive small cities of the state, where people smile easily and respond quickly to a friendly smile, where life takes a bit of a slower pace yet lies astride of the mainstream of busy events of the bustling San Joaquin Valley. Gateway to Yosemite, it has earned its place in history.

Hall of Bear Mountain Lodge No. 76

This picture, a copy of one taken before 1898, undoubtedly shows this Lodge just as it has been, with minor changes, throughout the years since it was purchased in 1869.
Here, it is thought, Brother Samuel T. Clemens, author of Mark Twain's Famous Jumping Frog of Calaveras, visited at various times as he tramped the Mother Lode Hills. This Lodge has never sustained a serious fire; its home looks much like the above, today.

BEAR MOUNTAIN LODGE NO. 76
and OPHIR LODGE NO. 33

Perhaps an injustice is perpetrated upon these Lodges with such unblemished records, to lump them together, yet it is not because of space or time that we do so. They exist within nine miles of each other and have at this very day a joint Trestle Board for their mutual benefit, and Ophir Lodge being one of the few "travelling Lodges" could actually have met in a private home within four miles of Bear Mountain Lodge No. 76 at one time, as their Charter so provides.

To unscramble them, let us consider the elder first. Ophir No. 33 was permitted under its Dispensation early in 1853 to meet anywhere within five miles of Murphys, in Calaveras County, and it was also a Moon Lodge meeting in the full of the moon rather than on a fixed date. In ninety years it had but two Treasurers, Riley Senter, forty-two years and M. H. Manuel, forty-eight years.

Miners and lumbermen, over its one hundred and fifteen years of existence, have not always been paragons of virtue, even allowing for the vagaries of men of such varying backgrounds and for the constant vigilance to admit only those who measure up to the high standards imposed by a Masonic outlook on life itself; harken to the minutes of this foothill-of-the-Sierras Lodge when we read the following: "A Lodge of Master Masons was opened in due form when the Worshipful Master stated that one Brother Francisco Rosa had violated his obligation as a Master Mason by getting money from different Lodges and spending it in houses of ill fame, when it was resolved by the Lodge that San Joaquin, Mokelumne Hill and Columbia Lodges should be notified forthwith of this conduct."

Bear Mountain, the younger of the two, is located in Angel's Camp, of jumping frog fame, and unlike many another old Lodge of the Mother Lode, has never sustained in all its history, a fire. No record remains concerning its acquisition of two very unusual Steward's Rods, which undoubtedly would have perished, as indeed others may have done, for they are made of solid silver. They lift, when grasped, like a heavy weight, and when released, don't bounce on the floor as a pool cue would, but thump, I was about to say, waking the dead.

Bear Mountain Lodge, almost on the slopes of a mountain of the same name, has not always through the years had the best time of it. Located on a slope facing the city of Angel's Camp that was founded in 1849, it is almost opposite the Angel's Hotel where Mark Twain first heard the story of the Jumping Frog. The hotel was first a mining camp necessity and erected with a canvas roof, then became one of wood, later one of stone, of one story in 1855, the second story added in 1857.

As I say, Bear Mountain Lodge has not always had clear sailing. The lean years, those that, as the saying goes, separate

The old door of Bear Mountain Lodge No. 76 has been replaced by this hand carved door of two-inch native sugar pine from adjacent hills of the Sierra Nevada. The past master who carved it learned the art from his father, an early member of this Lodge.

Modern downtown Sonora, County Seat of Tuolumne County, and home of one of the oldest Lodges in California, Tuolumne No. 8, is the southernmost largest, along with Mariposa, center of mother lode trading. Before 1870 Tuolumne No. 8 has been razed by fire at least three times; its current building, purchased in that year, now boasts a modern front as it, too, was consumed by flames, but lives on as a vigorous community asset.

Who would suspect that this modern front hides a ninety-year-plus Lodgeroom? Its two-foot thick walls fell into the street in the fire of 1927 but indestructible Tuolumne Lodge No. 8 has made a comeback typical of the mother-lode ingenuity through the years.

The home of one of the earliest Lodges, Tuolumne No. 8, Sonora is now almost a "boom-town" with a steady useful growth. Here was the Lodge, erected in 1852 or thereabouts and constructed of adobe, that "melted away in the rains."

the men from the boys, were also in evidence. One of the outstanding Past Masters of Masonry, from the standpoint of any Lodge at all, Spaulding Blood, was of most tenacious temperament. Many the year, as Master, he sat on the stone steps facing the valley, or ravine, as the mountaineers call them, and hailed a passing member to get his approval for paying the bills, as there was only the Master himself present at this particular stated meeting.

Bear Mountain Lodge is one in which, when one enters, Masonry comes alive and lives again, as one approaches that Great Light upon its altar. Its membership stands today at 83, a shining example of what faith and hard work can do. Mellow and dignified, it wears its new paint shining in the springtime sun, looking to a future of promise and usefulness.

TUOLUMNE LODGE NO. 8
and COLUMBIA LODGE NO. 28

No region of the gold fields of 1848 has attracted more attention than the region around Sonora, Columbia, and Chinese Camp. The place names of Second Garrote, Don Pedro's Bar, Jamestown, not to mention Jackass Hill and Mark Twain would be sufficient to entice most any interested person to tour the region and write about it. Many have, many more will.

At first glance, the Masonic record in the area may appear to the casual observer, at the least, confused. Tuolumne No. 8 itself has absorbed by consolidation two Lodges, Columbia Lodge No. 28 at Columbia, now restored by Grand Lodge as a showplace in Columbia State Park, 1891; the George Washington No. 62 at Chinese Camp, and because of rivalry between the communities, St. James No. 54 surrendered its charter rather than consolidate. Mountain Lodge No. 82 at Don Pedro's Bar was wiped out by fire in 1860 along with literally the entire mining community.

Samuel T. Clemens, who was just one of the boys nobody had ever heard of in particular, was a mining buff of sorts and lived in a cabin on Jackass Hill between Jamestown and Sonora. He was a Master Mason and a member of Polar Star Lodge in Missouri. It is quite possible and even probable that he visited Tuolumne Lodge No. 8 on various occasions. But if you wish to see the name on the books, you must take a vacation and do some avid searching, for it was not until long after the Civil War that Tiler's Registers began to be kept; before this, visitors were noted in the Secretary's minutes — sometimes — and many of the minute books have been lost through the years.

It will take much more research, and a braver man than your host in this little volume, to make any rash statements concerning Mark Twain. But it is my personal opinion, for what it may be worth, that although he panned unmercifully all organized religion as well as gold because of its man concocted dogmas, he was a believer in a Supreme Being, and one other Lodge nearby states flatly that he was appointed Junior Deacon all one winter.

Anyway, Tuolumne Lodge No. 8 was chartered on November 27, 1850. Yet only six months later in rendering its returns it showed the name of but one officer on its rolls, the Worshipful Master, C. M. Radcliff. One can but sympathize with Grand Lodge in its raised eyebrows over this, as the roll showed ten Master Masons, one Entered Apprentice with six other EA's withdrawn. This was May 1851. In November 1851 the return showed things back to normal; a full complement of officers with forty-six Master Masons on the roll. What had happened?

Really, two things had happened. First, many had disappeared into the gold fields. Next, some enterprising brethren had built themselves a new Lodge Hall. Fire being an ever present danger, the new hall was made of adobe, but the builders omitted the stone base and rubble and made the eaves too short, so that at the first deluge the base of the building crumbled and the whole structure became, as the historian Sherman states in his Fifty Years of Masonry in California, "a magnificent monument of mud" which soon washed away, "leaving a few particles of placer gold" scattered about. The fair weather masons simply vanished.

The next building was built of wood, and just as you surmise, it was burned to the ground in 1854. About this time a gentleman came to Sonora by the name of Baer and founded a clothing store. His son became a member of the fraternity in the again rebuilt Hall of 1870 which, along with his grandson, survives to the present time. The grandson is Marcel Baer, Past Master, and is the owner and operator of Baer's Clothing in Sonora at the present time. The Lodge stands intact now these 98 years.

The worshipful who submitted the returns with his own the only officer's name on the rolls subsequently became Most Worshipful Grand Master Charles M. Radcliff of the Grand Lodge of California, and it is this same Radcliff who was the chief engineer of the first steamship ever to enter the Golden Gate—The California, on February 28, 1849. He was, of course, a Scotsman.

As if Tuolumne No. 8 had not covered its ancient records with enough glory, it then enfolded within its sacred halls another to be Grand Master, who, although born and raised in Georgia, became a Captain in the National Guard of California. Upholding the Union cause of the war between the states, M. W. William Wilson Traylor became the second Pillar of old Tuolumne No. 8. Every Lodge, as you know, must have two Pillars.

Just four miles distant in the bustling mining town of Columbia, the "Gem of the Southern Mines" and the roistering, much written about come-hell-or-high-water-I'm-going-to-get-rich-community, was beginning to roll. In May of 1853 a Charter was issued to Columbia No. 28. Not until forty-one years later did it consolidate its Charter with Tuolumne No. 8, after the mining fever had subsided and Columbia deserted for more lucrative diggings.

The stories of the members of this Lodge could fill many volumes so we must content ourselves with a few shining stars like the great Jim Coffroth, lawyer and speechifier extraordinary, orator, promoter, poet, and State Senator from Tuolumne County. A man who numbered his friends by the thousands, a man who was raised in Columbia Lodge No. 28 and became its Master, a man with a great sense of timing and humor, entering into the rough play and human foibles of his day with the greatest alacrity, but a man of whom we must be proud. For it has been men like James Coffroth who were self-reliant and strong; the backbone of a country like ours. Not only was Jim Coffroth a favorite of the miners, but he was a two-fisted drinker, yet one found him solidly lined up on the side of law and order, and right motives. Yet, withal, he possessed a mighty sense of humor. Like the time of Paddy Farley's goats.

Patrick Farley, his wife, Maggie, and their two daughters, Mary and Annie, were without question shanty Irish. (May my ancestors, God rest their merry souls, forgive me.) They lived across the main gulch at Columbia along with many another of the same ilk. Others had pigs and chickens, the Farleys had goats, and it was their custom to let them roam the neighborhood. Goats love new succulent vegetables. They are smart, just like wild deer, who have relieved many a row of new beets of its sprouts as clean as a lawnmower. Paddy's goats roamed everywhere. One night one was caught, tied by its legs and dropped down the chimney of Farley's cabin, right into the living room ashes. Paddy was livid, got down

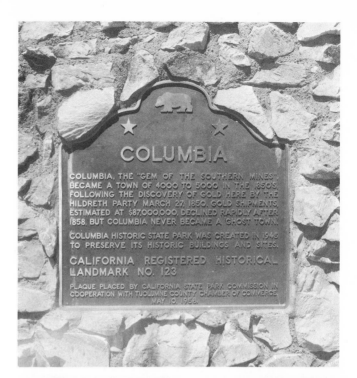

Somehow, the very texture of these bricks and stones of Columbia are reminiscent of the moil and toil of the thousands of miners who wrested from the earth the riches we all hope for.

Approaching a tenth of a billion dollars in gold, this Wells Fargo office in "downtown" Columbia handled this fabulous sum during the height of the "gold fever" days when men like Coffroth, Nugent, and Bulton were "top dogs" in Columbia town. Naturally, they also were members of Columbia Lodge No. 28.

his gun, until Maggie calmed him a bit.

Jim Coffroth one day was in the bar Paddy Farley & Co. had started at the lower end of town, joshing with Paddy's girl, Mary, who was forgetting to jot down the drinks, causing Paddy to make one of his remarks, stirring the ire of our hero.

Hearing about the goat incident, Big Jim Coffroth got together with his fellow lawyers, Nugent and D. C. Bulton, along with Judge Pendleton, the Justice of the Peace, and framed up a really good one on Paddy.

Coffroth appeared at the saloon with an official and enormous roll of paper from which he read to all and sundry a legal gobble-de-gook charging Patrick Farley and his wife, Margaret, with goat dereliction, requiring their presence in Judge Pendleton's court. Upon appearance, after suitable arguments, after suitable adjournment for drinks all around, after defense attorney Bulton had his say—(and lawyer Bulton was notorious for winning his cases)—that it was an outrage his clients should suffer disgrace and humiliation, the Judge rendered his decision: dismissal of the charges and damages from the city of Columbia to the tune of one hundred fifty thousand dollars. This was adjusted to pounds so that Paddy, who came to California by way of Australia, could understand three hundred fifty-seven pounds sterling. Like Bobbie Burns said, affairs of men, gang aft aglay.

Come Monday morning Paddy and Maggie and Mary and Annie are at Coffroth's office each with a basket to collect. Coffroth and Nugent explained that Columbia didn't have the money but would give them a judgement, further explaining that it would be just as good as gold "whenever you collect it." So they wrote it out, big seal and all. To this day the judgement is said to stand against the town of Columbia.

The stories of the Columbia years are legion, the pages of this little account, numbered.

For 36 years the Masons of the "Belle of the Southern Mines" met in a building of which this one, at the entrance to Columbia, is a replica. Maintained by the Grand Lodge of California, it is today a focal point for the edu- *cation of every visitor on the facts of life on what makes the Masons tick. The lower floor portrays a Museum of Masonic artifacts.*

CHAPTER III

ANCHORS OF THE SOUTHERNMOST BASTION

MARIPOSA LODGE NO. 24
and HORNITOS LODGE NO. 98

Without question the most important and famous building in the Mariposa community, this Mariposa Courthouse, erected in 1854 of local timber, is held together by mortise, tenon and wooden pegs. The clock came round the horn in an early clipper.

The town of Mariposa is the home of the "Butterfly Lodge" Mariposa No. 24 which supports a colorful history. Her Lodge home burned in 1866. Today she is vigorously carrying on the tradition of the "good men and true."

Mariposa is the southernmost bastion of the mining district known as the mother lode, and Mariposa Lodge No. 24, called "The Butterfly Lodge," came into being May 5, 1853 and has enjoyed a colorful and interesting career, through good times and bad, nestling in the steeper foothills among the quartz outcroppings certain to insure much change and activity among men.

One could say this Lodge was born November 29, 1851, the same year that Yosemite Valley was discovered by members of the Mariposa Battalion of whose numbers five were members, and also two of whom were California Rangers, the famous company of twenty-five horsemen who pursued and terminated the rampages of that notorious bandit chief, Joaquin Murietta.

Two facts about Mariposa have always created interest to all the craftsmen wheresoever dispersed: one that it is a Moon Lodge and the other that it is a Roving Lodge. Moon Lodges, there are still several here and there up and down the state, had their stated meetings on a certain day after the full of the moon rather than on a fixed date in order that members could walk or ride horseback to and from meetings in the light of the moon. Mariposa was a roving Lodge in that it could, without dispensation, hold its meetings at any location within five miles of the County seat of Mariposa, in fact did, many times meet at Agua Fria, a town of about a thousand at one period, just within its five-mile limit, where its Secretary lived.

Another unusual event, just a year after its founding was the presentation to the Lodge by thirteen Master Masons' wives and daughters, a Holy Bible, a solid silver square and compass, all in use now in this present day.

When the present munificent edifice was complete, that jewel set upon Nob's hill in San Francisco, and the old and august body known as the Most Worshipful Grand Lodge of Free and Accepted Masons of the State of California, took up its gavel for the first time, it was that stalwart secretary for twenty-seven consecutive years and Past Master of the Butterfly Lodge, Worshipful James P. McElligott who was first recognized from the floor.

Mariposa No. 24 through all her days to come, will be proud of that.

Unusual View of Mariposa County Courthouse

While County Government has carried on for 115 years in this grand old wooden building, Masonic Records, both from old newspaper files and from documentary records, are sparse. We wish we could say that one gleaned from the Mariposa Gazette for August 28, 1868 was one, but it did say that "Emerson (referring to Ralph Waldo Emerson) thinks himself fortunate when he can write 20 good lines in a day. The public thinks itself fortunate when it can understand one of them."

HORNITOS LODGE NO. 98

Maintaining its precarious existence under conditions that would long since have dissolved many a less determined group of brethren, Hornitos Lodge No. 98, having been granted a charter as Quartzburg Lodge No. 98 located some four or more miles distant, continues, in spite of the loss of the mining industry, to be one of our most colorful, and upon reflection of the reader must agree, most fruitful of Lodges. For it typifies the teachings of the ancient craft in its faithfulness to the purposes for which it was founded.

During gold rush days in the mother lode, fire was probably one of the dangers even more prevalent than the sudden storms of the Sierras, or the rush of the emotions of men afflicted with gold-fever bolstered with an itchy trigger-finger. From one end of the gold fields to the other the single most noticeable landmark that survives the decay of years, the march of progress, and the encroachments of the ever-present souvenir finder, is the large iron doors that decorate both preserved buildings and abandoned ruins flung across the country-side. These doors, while they undoubtedly did obstruct thieves in the night, had even a more important function—they were fire-doors. As such they contained many a fire until the bucket-brigade could be brought into play.

Fire came twice to Hornitos Masons, first at Quartzburg, when all was lost, and again at Hornitos. Mining, too, has a way of becoming exhausted. Hornitos, Spanish for "little oven," being no exception. Members dwindled away, but not one William Adams, who was raised in Hornitos Lodge in 1867 and learned his lessons well. He was installed the fourteenth Worshipful Master in 1872, and without pause continued as Worshipful Master until Brother Albert Hendricks became Master in 1901—a span of twenty-seven consecutive years, being reelected the twenty-eighth time, a record without parallel in Masonic history. Today Hornitos Lodge No. 98 boasts a membership of 107 and dispenses Masonic Charity as assiduously as it always has over its long history.

In no small part is this tenacity due to its present-day Masters and its Secretaries, notably its present one, now in his eighteenth year of tenure, a man of quiet demeanor, firm and dedicated to the age-old principles every Mason reveres. Walter Austin McCollum is no ordinary Mason, and will long be remembered for his towering strength of character. To some, the days of the big storm of 1938—or was it 1937 —that all but blew the roof from the Hornitos Temple, will be a day to remember. The story is brief, and I shall relate it just as Walt told it to me.

Masons have ever been more on the fewer side than on the side of quantity, which is by way of saying that every community of the mother lode also has its quota of people who are of that other faith. These folks around Hornitos have always been on the friendliest terms with the brethren. One day in 1937—or was it 1938—the wind blew with destructive force. It was the day the old hotel next door, long abandoned but now used as a storehouse for the road gang and their equipment belonging to the County Road Department of the County of Mariposa, blew down. The old two-story hotel was constructed of heavy brick, but on this late date its repair left something to be desired. The road gang sought shelter in it from the storm. At its height they noticed the tin roof of the Hornitos Temple next door was just preparatory to parting company with the rafters. Quickly they swarmed out of the old brick hostelry, and with fingers certain in their movements from long practice they detached several heavy blades of the road scraping machinery stored within, which they hoisted up to the roof, securely holding it in place, preventing a catastrophe just about as ruinous to its contents as would fire itself.

This was a generous act, certainly a quick-thinking act, on the part of these obviously non-Masons, but the sequel is astounding, and to some, will suggest the all-knowing Father's constant care and providence, for just as they were just putting the finishing touches to their missionary work, the building in which they were just sheltered collapsed and fell with a great swoosh. Had they been within its walls, all surely would have perished that day.

So the little Lodge at Hornitos still stands intact, all majestic 17½ by 30 feet of it, one of the smallest in the state. May its tribe prevail.

A Monument to Patience and Fortitude, Hornitos Lodge stands today proudly serene in its assurance of time-tested virtues of a bygone era.

Copied from a snapshot that is a prized possession of its Secretary, this is Hornitos Lodge as it appeared at an early day.

M.W. Leon O. Whitsell, P.G.M. (right) and M.W. James T. Frazer, P.G.M., stand before the old Lodge Hall at Hornitos. Taken about 1938 before the collapse of the building walls on the right during the "big blow." Copied from a snapshot in a private collection.

CHAPTER IV

THE LAND OF THE TULE

SAN JOAQUIN LODGE NO. 19
and MORNING STAR LODGE NO. 68

Present home of San Joaquin No. 19 and Morning Star No. 68. This modern building, built in 1921, boasts a real working day by day feature: a cafeteria, that is patronized by the Eastern Star and the Youth Orders, as well as its supporting Lodges, and is open to the public. Located in downtown Stockton, that almost became named Weberville after its founder.

As the crow flies, it is a little over a hundred miles from San Francisco Bay to the Gold Fields. About two-thirds or slightly less of that distance lies the city of Stockton, easily navigable by way of the upper San Francisco Bay, the Sacramento and the San Joaquin Rivers. No wonder Stockton became the transfer center for merchandise and goods going to the gold diggings, the home of an early Masonic Lodge, and what we might today call in polite circles a "rough neighborhood." It was here that the wagon trains under their wagonmasters, themselves a hardy breed, began their journeys whose destination was the boys up in the foothills.

Tradition has it that one Captain Weber, who had obtained a Spanish grant, founded the city of Stockton and made an agreement with Commodore Stockton for him to go east and obtain settlers, in return for Weber's agreement to call the city Stockton. Weber remained behind to administer its growth. San Joaquin Lodge came into being on May 5, 1852 with twenty-seven on its rolls as Master Masons. Considering its environment, a river town in the days of boom and bust, Adams Express and the gold shipments, it did well with only one suspension and two expulsions during a period of thirteen years through Civil War days.

Hot-heads and others of political bent were sure to add flavor and interest to a burgeoning society such as this. Its first Junior Warden was such a paragon of virtue as to fight a duel with the Master of Los Angeles Lodge No. 42 at Oakland on September 21, 1854. While both survived the ordeal, both were promptly expelled by their Lodges for un-Masonic conduct. Rasey Biven was a newspaperman and Warden of San Joaquin. Millard P. Dorsey, Worshipful Master of Los Angeles No. 42, was a fire-eating southerner. Biven was later restored to Masonic privileges.

17

For many years San Joaquin was a restless lodge. For want of a better word, restless is as good as the next. Bill Brown, member of No. 19, was anything but restless until Bill Bowlin, a desperado, threatened to kill him because he had testified against him in court. On the evening of April 1, 1853, Bowlin shot him as he crossed a bridge, jumped on his saddle horse and by a relay of horses fled to Mariposa County. Brother Brown died and citizens rallied to the largest funeral to that time in Stockton. The desperado, with $6,000 on his head offered by Governor Bigler, and another $1,000 by the Masons and Odd Fellows, swallowed a vial of prussic acid as the sheriff's posse neared him in the Mariposa hills.

Violence was a pastime in the frontier days, but we can be sure that the stabilizing influence of the citizens who stood for doing the right thing, and for law and order, were not far from the meeting halls of a Masonic Lodge.

Speaking of being a restless lodge, in about seventy years this lodge has had seven different meeting places. From a plain brick building in a gambling saloon that boasted only wood floors and a small coal stove, with a few wooden benches, to a newly carpeted and automatically heated temple, San Joaquin Lodge No. 19 has survived the years. In its day it was custom for this Lodge to hold Mock Funerals. The first was for U.S. Senator Henry Clay in 1852. Later one was held for Abraham Lincoln who, even though not a Mason, it was felt was entitled to every consideration. One was held for President McKinley.

In 1897 the brethren of San Joaquin Lodge had something, for that day, to talk about. Their Temple Association Director, Brother Joseph D. Peters, a faithful member for over forty-one years, had asked for a demit. He wanted it, he said, that he might be in communion with the Roman Catholic Church.

A Lodge that can withstand defection, shootings, chicanery, fire, and survive with a finest of records for its charitable spirit, is no ordinary Lodge. San Joaquin, true to its name, which translated means the establishment by the Holy Lord Jehovah, will prevail, and transmit to future generations, yet unborn, the fruits of its Masonic Labors.

MORNING STAR NO. 68

While the outside stairway leading to the third floor of the Weber House in Stockton may have been slippery and treacherous, the steps taken by Morning Star Lodge No. 68 were firm and purposeful. It organized soon after its mother Lodge, San Joaquin No. 19, was fully in operation. Yet it took but six days for the then Grand Master in Sacramento, Most Worshipful Brother William M. Howard, to issue a dispensation, December 14, 1854, and at the sixth annual Communication of the Most Worshipful Grand Lodge to grant a charter on May 4, 1855.

A Moon Lodge, like many of the period, was quite usual, because street lamps were few and far between, but the arrival of the brethren in boats to attend a regular communication of the Lodge in January of 1862 after a real downpour was anything but usual. In California the unusual is sometimes usual.

It is customary, however, for Morning Star to attract important people. Like John M. Buffington, for instance, who came across the Isthmus of Panama arriving on the steamer Oregon, who settled in Stockton and became one of its most prominent citizens and builders. Initiated in San Joaquin No. 19, he had many friends who helped found Morning Star. So he petitioned to receive the second and third degrees in the new Lodge. He became Alderman and Mayor of the City of Stockton, went on to become Superintendent of Public Schools in San Joaquin County. Brother Buffington became

School Director and Inspector of Elections in San Francisco. He removed to Oakland where he served as President of the Young Men's Christian Association. He assisted in establishing many of the higher bodies of Masonry in our State, and lived to become an honored and respected holder of the thirty-third degree of the Scottish Rite.

These early years were times of testing and trial, just as are the years of our own times. Men of stature and great worth have graced the annals of Morning Star Lodge. Two of popularity and fame came to mind.

One who simply carried out the routine matters that occur in every well-ordered organization was Austin Sperry, who was elected Treasurer. He served from 1858 until 1862. His occupation was that of miller, and he built himself a small mill in Stockton where his business flourished, and said business became the forerunner of the world-famous Sperry Flour Company, creators of mountains of bread, hills of cake, islands of doughnuts.

The other brother is even more widely known, or was, up until the past few years. His name was I. Whitney Lyons, and his profession was that of dentistry. In December of 1856 when Dr. Lyons left Stockton, his calling had not reached the pinnacle of prestige with which we accord dental surgeons of today. Dr. and Bro. Lyons had been making his own toothpaste for his clientele in Stockton, and you guessed it, when he went east he struck it big, for he became the originator of the famous Dr. Lyons Tooth Powder.

No account of Morning Star Lodge would be complete without the full, even if condensed, account of the life and affairs of Ruel Colt Gridley, who joined Morning Star Lodge No. 68 on May 23, 1867, being "late of Austin Lodge No. 10, Nevada." His fee for affiliation was donated to him upon his election, for he was already famous and endeared to a grateful nation.

It all started in Nevada at Austin during the Civil War. Losing a bet, his penalty was to carry a sack of flour a mile and a half all uphill. Decorated with red, white and blue flags and ribbons, he complied, the town band the while playing "John Brown's Body Lies a Mouldering in the Grave."

At journey's end what to do with the flour? Bro. Gridley offered to auction it off for the Sanitary Commission, precursor of the Red Cross. The successful bidder returned it to him for re-auctioning, and several auctions later a considerable amount had been raised.

Shouldering the sack, he trekked to other Nevada towns. The idea caught on. He came to California, then toured the Eastern States. The last auction brought $15,000 and a total of $275,000 was raised for relief of Civil War sick and wounded.

In all this, Brother Gridley ruined his health. Returning to Stockton, he and his family lived penniless in the camping areas among the tules which seemingly covered for miles the marshes and low-lying lands around the townsite outside the settlement. He hobbled in on crutches every day to scrounge for simplest necessities for himself and his wife, the former Susan Snyder of Missouri. Then he moved into a two-room house, and about this time it was learned he was a Master Mason in good standing. People were shocked when they learned his real identity. A subscription of popular nature was taken up to provide a home, food, and clothing.

His comeback was impressive. He became postmaster of Paradise City in Stanislaus County, and lived as a leading merchant there until 1870.

The Grand Army of the Republic, veterans organizations of Civil War fame, erected a monument showing Brother Gridley standing with his hand on a sack of flour. The original sack, still decorated with ribbons and flags, now reposes in the Nevada Historical Museum in Reno, Nevada.

Thus the years roll, in Lodges like Morning Star. Other greats have graced its halls. Others will.

"And many came, not to spoil, but to do good and be better, for in this environment men of principle soon rose above the gold of the mountains and the grass of the valleys, to seek the Great Light from above."

Gridley and his sanitary flour was well known during the Civil War. This monument, erected by the Grand Army of the Republic, the "American Legion" of the latter nineteenth century, honors Brother Ruel C. Gridley for his persistent faithfulness to an ideal. An ideal that, incidentally, helped to raise over a quarter of a million dollars (about two million now) for the war relief on behalf of the Sanitary Commission, national forerunner of the American Red Cross. His masonic career is almost as intriguing as his flour exploit, to be found in the narration of Morning Star Lodge No. 68.

CHAPTER V

"AMADOR IS DIFFERENT"

AMADOR LODGE NO. 65 and
HENRY CLAY LODGE NO. 95

Even the casual Mason who reads these lines may become surfeited with the sameness we encounter in recounting the fables and foibles of the gold-inspired Lodges of the Mother Lode.

But not with Amador. From the time one can remember being a part of their adjacent community to the north, Amador has been a community apart. Where else can one find Italian descendants of the time of Garibaldi? Where else can one find the mother church of a continent, St. Sava's Serbian Orthodox Church, constructed in 1894? Where else can a Lodge, say Amador No. 65 located in the County Seat of Jackson, tick off on its fingers names like Spagnoli, Moretto and Giusto? And like Barbarini, Caminetti and Chichizola? Yes, and like Pelluomini, Bagneschi, Michelotti and Giannini? And in Henry Clay Lodge No. 95 Dan Ramazotti is easily as good as Harry Byrd would be in the State of Virginia.

From Jackson to Sutter Creek is four miles. Now do you see why these two Lodges are teamed up together? Not only because of their physical closeness but because Amador is not only a County, it is a state of mind; and one cannot properly separate these two groups any more than an Amador man can be separated from the Italian Society Picnic Grounds situated just midway between the two towns at Martell.

The County of Amador has been a lively place since its founding and that was about 1848. From the time the stopping place by the side of the spring began to collect the cast-off bottles until the settlement which sprang up thereabouts and was called Botellas, to the present day one finds a lively air stirring about the City of Jackson, its County Seat. People of this ancestry play, work and live with zest, and I am not speaking of soap. I am speaking of the "speakeasies" of the early twenties, of the slot machines with the handles that

sometimes for three cherries gave out nickels that I personally pulled as late as the year 1952. If one knew the right spot in which town to go, that is. I am speaking of the "wide open" aspects right on down from the day when the Honorable Marion William Gordon in 1851 persuaded the Legislature to separate Amador County from Calaveras. This after a knock-down-drag-out fight over balloting that is a classic even in the rough and tumble of the great western migration. I am speaking of the fact that even to this hour automobiles with white doors, if you know what I mean, gather in twos and threes in this vicinity, perhaps not without reason.

But the territory of Amador County is no trollop. Her citizens are as law abiding and as patriotic and as peace minded as the best anywhere. It is only that there is an éclat about her that attracts attention, makes life seem vital, fresh and alive. Her sons are as honored as any. James T. Farley, later a U.S. Senator, joined Amador No. 65 in 1869 after withdrawing from another Amador County Lodge, and returned to Jackson where he died in 1886. Samual B. Axtell, a native Ohioan, came to Amador in 1851 and later became the first Governor of New Mexico, and called to order the first Grand Lodge, A.F. & A.M. of that jurisdiction. Divot Benedetto Spagnoli joined Amador Lodge about 1860, and after serving as County Clerk was appointed Consul at Milan, Italy, by President Cleveland. And there was Anthony Caminetti who served several terms in the State Senate of California and was appointed Commissioner of Immigration by President Woodrow Wilson.

Amador's sons, as well as those of neighboring Sutter Creek, are as illustrious as all those hardy breed of brothers who brought a vast continent to terms, mainly by their bare hands, agile brains, and a firm trust in God that nothing could shake.

The stories that are rife in this region are legion. Some are verifiable, some are not. Those that are not are usually brief, change their details often and go about like this: an unruly brother was always putting black balls in the box. It got so bad we could scarcely get a good man in to work on, the raconteur relates. Finally we thought of something to fox old "George" or old "Sam" as the case may be. Seems as though George (or Sam) had an old shack out behind his barn he used to keep his tools, plow, and spare harness in. One night just before Lodge one of the boys made some special arrangements. Sure enough, when we balloted same old black one showed up. Just then some one hollered, "There's a fire out there" and sure enough it was George's old shack. George made a beeline for home, and then is when we had another ballot taken. Whether this was Amador No. 65 or or Henry Clay No. 95 we are not sure.

Those that are verifiable are either in the minutes or are such a part of the history of the Lodge in question, that all details match and are held in the highest repute.

As an example, the minutes of Henry Clay Lodge on September 9, 1907 show that a certain candidate was prepared and introduced. When a certain interrogation was propounded soon after his entrance, his answer was far from satisfactory. The Worshipful Master, desiring that there be no question or doubt that the candidate fully understood the question, repeated it in what the minutes called a "decidedly comprehensive form." The second reply of the candidate being manifestly at variance with our well-known requirements and there being no doubt of his state of mind, he was taken out of the Lodge Room in a manner strictly in accord with Masonic usage precisely in the form known only to Masons.

Another example, and probably more humorous, that happened in 1890 has to do with the presentation of an apron when it was found that there was no apron to present. Whereupon the candidate was presented with a "make-do" apron prepared upon the spot from a borrowed bedsheet of a nearby hotel with the promise that the Lodge would in future see that he obtained a better one. In September 1931, when this candidate was a Past Master of this Lodge, such presentation was made "in fulfillment of a promise made over 40 years ago."

Has the reader ever heard of a tribute member? Well, we had them in plenty in the days previous to 1885 when Grand Lodge ended the practice involved. Many brothers who came to the gold fields brought their demits with them. Their own Lodges back east furnished them readily as conditions were far different in that far day of slow travel and slower action, although sometimes when I see our non-affiliated brethren in our midst who ought to affiliate, I wonder. Owing to the transitory nature of their work they hesitated to affiliate, but always did deposit their demits with the Secretary and paid Lodge dues just like a regular member. Then when ready to pull up stakes and go to another "diggin" for perhaps better luck, the Secretary handed back their demits from their original Lodge and they were "free to travel." Henry Clay Lodge and Amador Lodge had many of these valued brethren.

Before 1960 it was the custom to appoint investigating committees in open Lodge and for them to report back in the same way—in open Lodge. At one period Henry Clay had an "epidemic of rejections" and among these one stout-hearted hopeful was not to be put off. He received his first rejection and one year later to the day was back with another application. This too, was rejected. He waited a year, or perhaps two, and was turned down a third time, but the fourth was accepted and all seemed clear, everyone concerned breathing a sigh of relief, you can be sure.

The date was set for his reception. The candidate was in waiting and I am sure you are already telling me what happened. There was another objection. Twenty years after his application, this brother was received, and in due course, became a Master Mason in his Lodge.

In Amador City, just a whoop and a holler up the road from Sutter Creek, alongside the highway at a spot where the road turns sharply, there is a cemetery. In May of 1856, when Henry Clay Lodge received its Charter, it was a resting place for many of our pioneer Californians, and in this Lodge at this time was one Albert H. Rose, who, when he died, possessed some peculiar notions of preservation for those he loved. Being affluent, he arranged to have a beautiful vault constructed of sturdy brick. It held two places, one atop the other, all being constructed above ground. The lower berth, so to speak, was made to hold a metal casket in which was

With a modern dress, here stands old Amador Lodge No. 65 at the corner of Broadway near Main, Jackson. Just across the street in the building, next to the Wells Fargo Restaurant, is the tallest, it is said, three-story building in the world. The embrasures of the windows of the Masonic Building in the foregoing reveal its great age, probably around Civil War time.

placed a valve to admit the addition of alcohol, for the body was steeped in that fluid, and the terms of the will stipulated that once a year the alcohol be replenished. The bottom section held the remains of his dear daughter, while the upper space was for our Charter Member himself, Albert H. Rose. In the course of events both were occupied. Finally, we must suppose, the money of the will, as these legacies do, ran out. Time was also stroking his beard, or perhaps stroking the ringlets of the virgin's hair, as the years rolled on.

Now we are well into the twentieth century. Three things of this story remain, the old cemetery long forgotten and moss grown, and the two Masonic Lodges of Amador County, Henry Clay No. 95 and Amador No. 65.

On a certain day of 1958 a logger with a rig fitted with a low bed truck and hauling a huge caterpillar tractor swung around the brow of the steep hill just above Amador City. He gained speed as he swung the corner. Lightly he touched the powerful stream of the air-brake. No response. Harder. No response. With all his might he clung to the wheel as the inevitable occurred. Hospitalized but alive was the driver, after the rig had split open a wide swath into an old cemetery ripping out one whole side of an above-ground vault. In the bottom layer, nothing. The ravages of time had taken their toll. In the upper, a perfectly preserved little man, all in frock coat, white shirt, string tie, and the finest little goatee you ever did see.

These are the histories of Lodges that live on to become the strength and support of our America. But I won't bore you with them all, perhaps some future historian will uncover from the ancient scrolls all of their perfume and flavor. Before we leave the entrenched gold of Amador County, one parting shot. How many of you are familiar with Sky Rights as pertain to a Masonic Lodge Building? No one? Yes, I thought perhaps I had you there. Therein lies a tale.

In the early days, Henry Clay Lodge No. 95 and I.O.O.F. Lodge No. 31 purchased a building in Sutter Creek on the main drag. Each was to own an undivided third of the ground and "that part of the building occupying said ground is owned by others than the Fraternal Bodies" recited the deed. Henry Clay's right *begins* "where the first floor structure *ends in height* and can be built to the heavens if they so desire." There has been quite a furor from time to time concerning this most unusual arrangement—but then up here in Amador what's a few "Sky Rights" among friends?

The despair of every antiquarian who has ever beheld it,
this Lodge Hall dating to pre-Civil War days is yet today
the every-month meeting place of Volcano Lodge No. 56,
Amador County, California. Both the Charter to this
Lodge and to I.O.O.F. Lodge No. 25 were received in
1854-55. On the second floor, below, was the editorial and
printing offices of the weekly Ledger. Pedestals and altar
arrived on a sailing vessel coming around Cape Horn.
Carpet and seats are modern, chairs originals.

CHAPTER VI

THE UNERUPTING VOLCANO

The continuing dedication of men like William W. Leon, P.M., Secretary of Volcano Lodge No. 56, that is equal to the best that has characterized this foothill Lodge from the beginning. Shown here is the cave where early organizational meetings were held. The site, and the rock formation and grounds surrounding it, now owned by the Lodge is open to tourists, daily.

The town of Volcano is one of those places in the mother lode that has survived despite its usefulness having departed for other climes. One should say, almost survived, for today it is but a memory and a tourist center receiving those who flock here to see the old St. George Hotel, and listen to the tales of the early mining days.

The town itself nestles in a beautiful setting of tall pines and deciduous growth of oak and locust. It lies in a small valley along Sutter Creek that furnished millions of dollars in gold, very welcome to Abraham Lincoln in his struggle to hold the Union together. Over one of the widened-out spots in the creek bed an up-thrust of rock provided a series of caves. In the roistering days when gold and whiskey, shooting and general hell-raising prevailed, a number of Masons got together in one of those caves to hold their first few meetings.

Afterwards, they erected a building atop this rock escarpment to house Volcano Lodge. This building burned, and the Lodge moved to the present stone and mortar building where for more than one hundred years it has somehow survived the ebb and flow of humanity.

A few of the foundation stones of the earlier building remain. The Lodge has of recent date been able to purchase this site, and with remarkable perseverance and industry is preparing to preserve its salient features for future generations. The old cave, where early brothers met under most adverse conditions, is now open to public view with a caretaker in attendance.

Reduced in membership during the long lean years to a mere handful of perhaps eighteen or less, this grand old Lodge now carries on its roll one hundred and twenty-seven members. They meet in a hall hallowed and preserved intact in its nineteenth century dress, every piece of furniture a priceless antique, every chandelier equipped for kerosene or candle, a delight to the collector's eye.

Many important men have graced its meetings, its members early dispersed far and wide to become famous in their own right. Men like Dr. Washington Ayer who graced the San Francisco scene as a top flight administrator, and James T. Farley, later U.S. Senator. Even the very streets of San Francisco have been named for brethren who graced the rolls of Volcano Lodge, such as Ross and Berry, Howard and Harrison.

Many are the stories that grow out of years of occupancy of a mellowing institution such as Volcano Lodge No. 56. Its canopy that shelters the East, an item evident in many another of the older Lodges, consisting of velour drapes held in a tie-back forming a covering that gives the feeling of both elegance and the throne of a far eastern potentate, dominates the East of Volcano's Lodge Hall. One of these stories has to do with the enormous rat that was wont to sit at its apex viewing with quiet dignity all the ceremonies taking place in the dimly lighted scene below. Another story, which is quite easily verifiable, has to do with calling off a degree conferral long enough for the stewards to chase out of the hall several of the quite rare family of mammals capable of true flight, the common bat.

How Volcano came to acquire its name is lost in the mists of time. True, the geographical configuration of the townsite suggests such a name, but there is little evidence that it was in reality, such. There is much more validity in the antecedents of the old town jail built in the 1870's. It stands just across the narrow street from the Masonic Hall and of itself attracts but little attention. Its appearance belies its age and importance. It certainly does not demean itself as a true relic of the past until the closest scrutiny. It is but one story tall, and being of weathered planks standing vertically, one's interest lags until it is pointed out that between this outer two inch plank and a similar one within, lies sandwiched between a layer of good old boiler plate.

The story is that the two gentlemen who had the pleasure of constructing this bit of Americana had the extreme pleasure of being its first two inhabitants. There is no record of their ever escaping. Since the whole jail measures only twelve by sixteen feet—as I stepped it off in this year of our Lord—we also doubt they became frayed from excessive exercise during their enforced vacation.

The larger two-story stone structure which is also the home of I.O.O.F. Lodge No. 25, just across the roadway, built in 1854, is the home of a Masonic Lodge that history and time cannot erase. In the capable hands of present-day Masons who value its place in the scheme of things, we know it will extend its benignant rays into a bright and shining future by illuminating the paths of future Masons yet unborn.

Erected in 1854, this building has been the home of Volcano Lodge well over 100 years since the Lodge's original Home burned which was located atop the old cave rock in the river bed.

CHAPTER VII

THE VALLEY OF THE IONE

IONE LODGE NO. 80

Ione Valley is a beautiful spot in the Sierra foothills and comprises "Township Two" of Amador County. Ione Lodge No. 80 would probably have been a much lower number had it not been for a matter of eighteen dollars that the Lodge owed to the Grand Lodge which delayed the issuance of Charter and instead of an expected number thirty notches lower they received their present number 80.

People, even good Christian people, and good Hebrew people, or just any good people, never forget a thing like this. For years it was, and is to this day, a topic of discussion when old timers get together. Speaking of low numbers, it reminds me of a certain game played out of doors by the Scotsman, and I am told, by many Americans as well. But for well over the hundred year mark, number eighty has served Ione Lodge very well, indeed, be it high or low.

Probably named after a character in a legend, and not for the Greek Ionia, nor yet after one of the ancient and original orders of architecture, the Ionic, Ione was at first called by some decidedly inelegant names. First is was called Bedbug. Then it was called Freezeout. Not until six years after gold was discovered at Drytown, a matter of ten or eleven miles, was the yellow metal a factor at Ione.

Masonic meetings in this fertile valley were held until 1858 in a home at the corner of Church and Washington Streets, a building that is still standing and in use by a private family, one known through the years as the Reed house. In that year a hall was built that shows the regard of the fraternity for its public schools. Ione Lodge No. 80 completed that year a wood structure erected to be used as a grammar school on the ground floor and as a Masonic Hall on the second

Ione Lodge No. 80 met in this private residence until 1858 when they moved to their present building. Known as the Reed House, it is a landmark in the area, privately owned today, and is located at the corner of Washington & Church Streets, Ione.

floor. It later donated this building to the school district in its entirety after first placing it in a condition acceptable to the school board.

Civic pride has been one of Ione Lodge's first concerns. It made significant donations to completing the railroad when for want of funds the Central Amador Railroad reached a point outside town called Buckeye Station. One of its prime movers stands today near the City Hall as a souvenir of a glorious past, when choo-choos chuffed up the grades while a rancher's team of horses quivered with fright.

Ione Lodge was present at the cornerstone laying of the Preston School for Boys, a factor that looms great in the advancing civilization that is California. Begun with a handful of boys, this industrial school now cares for more than nine hundred young men.

A gold strike at Michigan Bar in the fifties created the usual community of eager workers, and as one might expect, there was sufficient of the stable element there to petition

Right Worshipful N. Curtis Greene, Grand Master Deputy for 1855 for a Dispensation, and in due course Nebraska Lodge No. 71 came into being. It held on as long as its founding center was viable, but after the mining faded away, it too faded, and in 1879 Ione Lodge No. 80 accepted this waif, by consolidation.

The permanent home of Ione Lodge came with the purchase of a two-story brick building adjacent to the Hall of the Native Sons of the Golden West, as half owner with the I.O.O.F. There is an odd condition in its connection, yet not as unusual as the other Amador oddity at Henry Clay Lodge in Sutter Creek. There, the first floor of the building is not owned by the Lodge, the second floor is. Here, in Ione, the only access to their Lodge Hall is by a stairway contained in an adjacent building, the Native Sons, and the ingress to their holding is by a door in the outside wall at second floor height, equipped with iron door, latch and all. As I have always said, "the things people do."

The building on the left houses Ione Lodge No. 80 and the one on the right the Native Sons of the Golden West. Well preserved and functioning as commercial establishments on the ground floors, they occupy the center of the Main Street of Ione City in Amador County. There is no access to one except through the other, on the second floors.

CHAPTER VIII

WHERE IT ALL BEGAN—GOLD! AT COLOMA!

EL DORADO COUNTY LODGES

GEORGETOWN LODGE NO. 25	ACACIA LODGE NO. 92
EL DORADO LODGE NO. 26	PALMYRA LODGE NO. 151
DIAMOND LODGE NO. 29	MT. ZION LODGE NO. 114
HIRAM LODGE NO. 43	PILOT HILL LODGE NO. 160

The town square at the "Tower" (left) in Placerville, familiarly known as "Hangtown" has had probably the most "colorful" history of any of the "dry diggings" of the lode country. Here is its Masonic Temple, built in 1893, still in use today. After earlier vicissitudes of fire, flood and languor, El Dorado Lodge No. 26 flourishes in the modern tide of empire.

People casually mention the length and breadth of California in many instances without actual experience of just how long and how wide it really is.

In the days of the gold-rush, it was, if anything, even longer and wider. The creaking of the bed, frame and wheels of a merchandise wagon going up a long dusty slope from Shingle Springs, the railhead, into Placerville, could take hours. The winding turns coming down the American River from Echo Pass into Riverton at the foot below Camino, could give the wagon driver a stiff back from constant pushing on the brake-lever with his foot to hold the wooden shoe against the wheel.

But as the pioneers got over the passes into California, many arrived in a destitute condition. Each Mason already there, and established in business, did his share to relieve this want. It was not long before many heard about the Grand Lodge being formed, and applied for admission. Georgetown being first, followed by El Dorado and Diamond Springs, and finally Hiram Lodge No. 43 at Mud Springs, later named El Dorado after the county.

If one could visualize the condition of affairs in the County of El Dorado in the middle eighteen fifties, it would be really simple to explain the shifting of the population, the organizing and abandoning of the various Masonic bodies, the consolidations, and the struggles for existence. El Dorado bears upon its rolls the members of three other Lodges. There was Mt. Zion Lodge located at Grizzly Flat which joined Palmyra Lodge in Placerville, a second Lodge in that city,

Hangman's Tree in Placerville, called "Hangtown," when Route 50 meandered through the city, was an eyefiller for tourists.

Taken a number of years ago, the Monument commemorates the founding, in 1859, by Mr. Sieg, of the first Grove of United Ancient Order of Druids in California.

The Ivy House Hotel behind it, was the favorite stopping place of Hank Monk, famous pioneer driver, and

Horace Greely of "Go West, Young Man," fame, in about the same period.

The view is of Main Street, at Cedar Ravine, looking Westerly in Placerville.

which itself joined El Dorado No. 26. Grizzly Flat is today one of the remotest spots in all California, although I won't argue the point, as I said this is still, for all our modern travel, a tremendous State.

The third Lodge to affiliate with El Dorado No. 26 was Acacia Lodge No. 92 at Coloma, organized in 1855, and until 1916 continued to uphold the tenets of Masonry in the town where gold first burst upon California.

No mention of Acacia Lodge or of Georgetown Lodge is complete without the mention of Thomas Milburne Read. It was he who assisted in organizing both Lodges and served both as Master. He became Treasurer of El Dorado County, member of the Board of Supervisors, and later in his life became a member of the Idaho Legislature and Grand Master of Masons in the State of Washington.

In fact all of these Lodges have been the breeding ground, the inspiration for many great men of California history, who figured large in Masonic history as well as political history, men of stature and substance, men who in every way did match the wonderful mountains with which they were surrounded. To list their names would require the full history of events that has been so ably presented by many a historian of Masonry, that space forbids us here.

And of course, too, we have had our scoundrels, yet so few are they, that one can almost write them up on the fingers of one hand, while our illustrious ones fill many volumes. Who but Past Master John Fisher of Hiram Lodge would persist in his devotion to a trust for so many years? For

This was the home of Acacia Lodge No. 92 chartered in May 1856. It is located at Coloma, El Dorado County, where gold was discovered. Now the home of the organization of the International Order of Odd Fellows, this old landmark should memorialize its glowing past for many more years under present State Park supervision.

On a slope above the South Fork of the American River at Coloma, in 1889, this Monument was erected to James Marshall. This old print was taken during the time that

Acacia Lodge No. 92 was flourishing in Coloma, destined to furnish California and Nevada with many important figures in Masonic annals.

The Old Temple at old Growlersburg (Georgetown No. 25) built by Shannon J. Knox from hand hewn, nailless supports and joists morticed together, was "home" to Masons from 1848 to 1948 when it burned, lighting tear-stained faces of laboring firemen who were its longtime members.

The new Masonic Temple built in 1950 by the dedicated members of Georgetown Lodge No. 25. This plant of concrete baselite block should serve this Empire County (El Dorado) Organization through many years to come in Georgetown, California.

This is the oldest building in constant use by the I.O.O.F. in the State of California. It was also the home of Diamond Lodge No. 29. Building was constructed in 1852. Its first Master, L. Bradley had a hand in laying out the wagon road from Placerville to Carson Valley, Nevada in 1856-7. The fire-hazard against the building shows why some at least of the early buildings are no longer standing.

twenty-three years he walked the railroad ties seven miles from Placerville to El Dorado to attend his Lodge of which he was Master for each of those long years.

There has been mention of fire in these pages as one of the terrors of the night to which the Mother Lode was subject. It is true that legends have grown up around them, coloring and adding to the original as legends are supposed to do.

Here is one that is told first hand by a Past Master of Hiram Lodge in which every spark is authenticated, for it happened to him. The year was 1923 and Dave Marks was then a quite young man. Near the town of El Dorado men were clearing land for a commercial enterprise. In that year bulldozers had not yet been developed, and land was cleared mainly by hand, by grub-hook and by pulley with horses. After clearing, the brush was piled to dry and later burned.

It was this later burning that became disaster for almost the complete village as well as Hiram Lodge No. 43.

An east wind arose that pushed the fire up a small ravine after which another wind change suddenly caught the dry grass and brush that sent the fire into town to demolish at least ten buildings, including the Church and the Lodge Hall. Passing up buckets was insufficient, as a bucket brigade is almost all of our Lode towns afforded.

Only the three-foot wall remained. Temporarily the Lodge went into the I.O.O.F. Hall at Diamond Springs where Diamond Lodge once met. Today Hiram Lodge is rebuilt, retaining its original walls and foundation, and carries on its growing roll a total of almost one hundred and fifty members.

Every Lodge of this El Dorado land has been demolished by fire at one time or another. However, No. 26 at the County Seat now has survived since 1893 when the present Temple was built, and in it a wonderful record of Masonry has ensued. It has been a center for the spread of principles hallowed by time and usage.

As the years swing by, and the progress of growth and change alter the face and character of not only the terrain but the habits and mores of the people who made this golden land their home, we know that the fruits of temperance, fortitude, prudence and justice will again prevail and make that difference from a lawless horde to a civilized group of prosperous and self governed Americans.

This is the rebuilt and restored building erected in the 1850s and was the home of St. James Lodge No. 54 in the rip-roaring mining days of the Mother Lode. Only four miles from Sonora, it indulged in rivalry that brooked no retreat. Jamestown today stands at the crossroads of progress or decay.

This old Masonic Cemetery at Jamestown, or "Jimtown" could tell many tales of Masonic brethren who died "far from home in a strange land." Even the Lodge, St. James No. 54 surrendered its charter after the mining became less attractive in the 1870s.

MASONIC HALL

UNDER DISPENSATION OPHIR LODGE NO. 33. F. & A.M., WAS PERMITTED TO MEET AT "EARLY CANDLE LIGHT" IN PRIVATE HOMES WITHIN A RADIUS OF FIVE MILES. THE LODGE WAS INSTITUTED IN JAN., AND CHARTERED MAY 6TH 1853. ORIGINAL, ONE-STORIED BUILDING ERECTED EARLY IN 1862. PRESENT HALL BUILT IN 1902. THIS IS ONE OF THE OLDEST LODGES IN STATE OF CALIFORNIA. IT HAS HAD BUT FOUR TREASURERS DURING ITS 95 YEARS OF EXISTENCE: B.B. WILKINS 2 YEARS, A.H. PUTNEY 5 YEARS. RILEY SENTER, 42 YEARS AND M.H. MANUEL NOW SERVING IN HIS 48TH YEAR.

In this "Early Candlelight Lodge" Ophir No. 33 was wont to label special meetings, "called meetings" adjourning to meet at a specified time. Such meetings opened without ceremony.

Today's view of the Cabin on Jackass Hill where it is said that Mark Twain and his cronies in the mining business were ensconsed during the gold rush. Clemens was a member of Polar Star Lodge No. 79 in St. Louis, Mo.

Built by the I.O.O.F. this building was shared by Calaveras Lodge No. 78 from 1856 until 1900, in this originally Mexican town of San Andreas. Fifty feet to the right of this photo, stands the Court House, now incorporated into another building, that held the trial of the famous bandit, Joaquin Murietta.

CHAPTER IX

AUBURN SAID EUREKA! FIRST

EUREKA LODGE NO. 16

These are Gold Rush Pioneers in Placer County. Taken in 1890, visualize their industry, courage and determination that made California great. See them as they were 40 years earlier. No. 5 is Geo. W. Applegate. No. 12 is Geo. Mitchell. No. 42 is Walter B. Lyons. All three were Masters of Eureka Lodge No. 16. Undoubtedly many more were members. Some names are unknown. Others are not members of the Fraternity. (Photo courtesy Calif. Fed. Savings & Loan Assn.)

The City of Auburn is a proud place. And not without reason. For Auburn is the largest and most prosperous and advanced community in all the mother lode. And I surely trust there will be no smoke, brimstone or fire issuing forth from other mother lode towns when I make such a plug for Placer County. Especially since we lived in the adjacent county to the south, and if you are not familiar with each, let us just come right out and say it is El Dorado.

Placerville is the County Seat of El Dorado County. Auburn is the County Seat of Placer County. How mixed up can one get? Well, in this case, there may be justification. Anyway, Auburn is the "Gem of the Northern Mines" if Columbia is the "Gem of the Southern Mines" and the "static" should be nominal from all and sundry.

The rich and interesting history of this region is ripe for many an interesting story. The one of how the American River received its name is simply a must. The Auburn area is one that just sprang into being after Marshall's gold discovery without any Spanish background. Well, almost. The Mexicans awoke to the fact that the American men were somehow filtering through the mountains from the East, and mainly by way of one river system that had three branches, so they named the river "El Rio de Los Americanos" which, of course, is the American River.

The first Masonic meeting occurred in July of 1851 at Eureka Bar on this same American River, where the miner in May of 1848 first exclaimed "eureka!" when he discovered he had the real McCoy in his pan. Like the vicissitudes of most of our Gold Rush fluidity of movement, the Masons were for a time in Eagle City on the middle fork of the river near Michigan Bluff before the Lodge was chartered and settled in Auburn on November 7.

It is a delight to peruse the history of Eureka Lodge No. 16 for while many another in the gold rush days were plagued by an occasional scoundrel in high places, Auburn seemed to exemplify the teachings of our Order to perfection. Without mentioning names or pointing the finger, at least two Lodges were purged by having their masters liquidated by expulsion; both were in the same county and both were the first Master of the Lodges in question. In this case the evil is interred with their bones and the good lives on. The only ripple in Eureka Lodge could be said to refer to Civil War days when the Secretary would write up his minutes referring to "Free and Accepted Ancient York Masons" which was a hallmark of the South, but nothing came of it. Considering the height of feeling in the 1860's, both before and after, the harmonious relationship maintained by the brethren is exemplary.

This does not mean that there were not unusual happenings in this as in all Lodges. There were. Small things, but enough out of the ordinary to engage our attention at this late day. Petitions for affiliation in an earlier day were received without much fuss or bother, being read and acted upon at the same meeting. In fact some were not even committed to paper; they were simply proposed by a brother, received and accepted and balloted upon then and there. On one occasion a brother was recommended by the Grand Matser, who was present, and he was accepted and elected to membership and then elected Worshipful Master all in the same evening.

An early practice that we might well adopt in our own time, with of course certain modifications, was that of writing a polite letter to a member asking him to "show the reason why he has not affiliated with the Lodge." The inferences here are many and are cogent. No Mason who is "worth his salt" should be footloose in a community without making his ties with the Lodge where he lives. Duties and responsibilities were not shirked by the good brethren of the era. Relief given

"In 1851 they located on the Middle Fork of the American River at a point known as Horseshoe Bend, a few miles from Michigan Bluff, in Placer County . . . where they built a safe Lodge room near a waterfall on the bank of the river . . . their meetings were attended by a large number . . . which afforded them all much pleasure." The Master of Eureka Lodge No. 16 then was Bro. Geo. Applegate. When mining waned and members drifted, he offered the charter to M.W. John A. Tutt, Grand Master, who refused it, so Bro. Applegate then settled in Auburn. Don't you think this a beautiful carpet?

to war funds, to assistance in times of flood and fire, and the good offices of Masons were never wanting in famine and fever or any calamity where suffering was apparent. Without intending to moralize we would undoubtedly do an even more creditable job today were we completely united into Lodges where we reside by edict of Grand Lodge than in sustaining the house divided condition that now prevails in our beloved jurisdiction of California, where the State motto itself is EUREKA. If we have "found it" let us acknowledge such by affiliation with our nearest brethren.

There could be no greater tribute to the brethren living and dead of Eureka Lodge No. 16 than the following lines attributed to Edgar A. Guest:

> I'd like to think when life is done
>   That I had filled a needed post
> That here and there I'd paid my fare
>   With more than idle talk and boast;
> That I had taken gifts divine,
>   The breath of life and manhood fine,
> And tried to use them now and then
>   In service for my fellow men.

Unsurpassed as a homeland from the days of '49 the City of Auburn flourishes as has no other gold crazed settlement of a century ago. This building is the modern plant of Masonic activity of Placer County, housing Eureka Lodge No. 16 whose members really "found it" November 7, 1851 when they were chartered by the Most Worshipful Deputy Grand Master John A. Tutt.

Soon after the frantic first gold rush days, when Auburn City of Placer County realized it would be more than the first rush of slab shacks and miners' tents—and other Chinese works of art—this is one of the main streets near its first plaza and the building nearest the top of the rise, on the left, was long the home of Eureka Lodge No. 16.

CHAPTER X

IN THE SHADOW OF THE HOLY CROSS

SANTA CRUZ LODGE NO. 38

This marker dedicates the Grove of Trees planted and dedicated to George Washington on the bicentennial of his birth, by Santa Cruz Lodge No. 38. It was in this Grove, located in the environs of Santa Cruz that the outdoor third degree was held.

Santa Cruz, as all will remember, is the home of the coastal redwoods, an especially beautiful part of California, swept by cooling sea-breezes, and early the locale of one of the chain of early missions of the Catholic Fathers who began their hegira in far-away San Diego.

As early as 1791, the Fathers built an adobe building to house the Mission Guard. The building is still standing today on School Street near the old Plaza. It is of interest to Masons for here, in the spring of 1853, was organized Santa Cruz Lodge, Free and Accepted Masons of the State of California. The story, if it could be told, would certainly be of interest, of just how it came about that we were accorded the privilege of using one of the then rather small village's quite private but most prominent buildings.

Be that as it may, on May 3, 1854 a charter was provided and a Lodge of 29 Master Masons came into being. And it has been a most active one.

One of its very first acts was to instruct the Secretary to inform all non-affiliated Masons that if they did not affiliate within three months, they would no longer be "considered available for Masonic Charities." And that, in that day and age, was cause for quite a bit of deep thought, for all Lodges of the era were very active in this matter, times being fluid and brethren relatively often being in need of assistance, which was always freely given.

For instance, there was the time a brother asked the Lodge to buy him a team and a conveyance. It was learned that the brother had a son in San Jose who was an attorney, a daughter who was a music teacher, and that the brother himself owned seven acres of land near Santa Clara.

The records state quite succinctly, "The Lodge decided the brother could buy his own team and buggy."

The first master of this Lodge, while under dispensation, was Henry G. Blaisdel. During the great silver excitement at Washoe in Nevada, he moved to Virginia City and became postmaster. Here, he found that our good brother, Most Worshipful William H. Howard, Past Grand Master of Masons in California, had become Sheriff of Storey County, in which Virginia City is located. Howard, an attorney, loved to play pranks. He arranged that when the court met the jury would be "hand picked" so to speak. One panel of jurymen were all "squint-eyed," another were all so corpulent they scarcely would fit in the jury box, and still another consisted of jurymen who were all in excess of six feet in height. Howard himself was six feet six inches in his stocking feet.

It is E. A. Sherman, who edited the edition of "Fifty Years of Masonry in California," to whom we are indebted for this story, and he mentions that the fees collected by these men were turned over to the Relief Society of Virginia City.

Many interesting bits of Americana have become a part of Santa Cruz Lodge, for this Lodge seems to have had from the earliest beginning a flair for entering the life of the community in which it was so much a part. In former days it was usual to open Lodge before a funeral, adjourn for the service, and close later. In 1861 a certain brother who had come to Santa Cruz died. When Lodge reconvened several brethren approached the East and deposited a black hardwood cane. It bore an inscription in circular form to A. W. Rawson, W.M. of Rawson Lodge No. 145 Illinois and bore an All Seeing Eye, a Square and Compass and A.L. 5854 enclosed in a circle. This cane was to be presented to Brother Rawson's son "at such time as he might become worthy of it by becoming a Master Mason." This latter event took place in 1870 and his son received the cane in accordance with the wish of his father.

The history of this coastal Lodge is studded with deeds of Masonic worth and meaning. Almost no year since its founding is without some anecdote or happening that would be worthy of a volume in which to record its many acts of

This pen and ink sketch on the left is the Old Adobe Birthplace of Santa Cruz Lodge No. 38 and on the right as it appears today. Erected 1791 to house the officers of Holy Cross (Santa Cruz) Mission Guard, it engenders many unanswered questions as to the apparent rapprochement between this early group of Masonic Brethren and the established Church of Santa Cruz.

charity, kindness, or activity worthy of the best that Masonry has to offer.

In the modern day again we find Santa Cruz Lodge not wanting. The nearby George Washington Memorial Park is the location for still another gift of these brethren, a grove of trees, now nearing a mature stand, and which was for several years the scene of an outdoor location for the conferral of the third degree. Benches were built into the side of the hill, and situated in the deep shade of the forest, with all avenues well guarded, the Lodge conferred the degree on its regular candidates in the presence of visitors from far and wide, some from as far away as San Francisco, about eighty-five miles distant.

While no longer possible to continue this novel way of impressing the candidate, the idea was one typical of Santa Cruz Lodge No. 38 which has always been in the forefront of every good activity of Masonic worth, living up to its hallowed name, Holy Cross, with a fervor worthy of those brethren who best can work and best agree.

This is 828 North Branciforte Avenue, Santa Cruz. It is the modern home of Santa Cruz Lodge No. 38 a justly proud group of Masons who have, for more than 100 years, served their community in closer union and purpose than many another. They constitute a vital factor in the life of Santa Cruz County.

Taken 15 years apart, this building was built by Santa Cruz Lodge No. 38 eighty-three years ago in 1886. The one on the left was photographed in 1952 or 1953, the one on the right in 1968. It served this Lodge well until their new Temple was constructed, is still a creditable and useful commercial asset to the community.

On the road to the "Mystery Trees" just outside Santa Cruz, this gate is the entrance to the Grove established by Santa Cruz (or Holy Cross) Lodge No. 38 to commemorate the two hundredth anniversary of Bro. George Washington.

In this secluded sylvan dell seats were constructed and Santa Cruz Lodge No. 38 for a number of years held outdoor third degree conferrals, until they became so popular they could no longer contain all those Master Masons who desired to witness it and was discontinued. It is located in the heart of the George Washington Memorial Grove.

CHAPTER XI

SO NEAR AND YET SO FAR

GOLD HILL LODGE NO. 32 and
NATOMA LODGE NO. 64

Ignoring the early crop of figs on the fig tree at the right, and visualizing the propper-up fence as being across the street, not against the building, this active Odd Fellows Hall has been long the home of Gold Hill Lodge No. 32 chartered in 1853. Have you elsewhere than in Lincoln in Sacramento County seen a building whose time clock is ten-of? Look again.

Gold Hill Lodge No. 32 is located in the town of Lincoln, a crossroad community on the road to Marysville at the point where the travel intersects it on their way to the goldfields. That at least was the case on May 6, 1853 when a charter was issued to the Lodge at a point about ten miles distant called Gold Hill. As the mining became less and less, the Lodge removed to Lincoln, already showing signs of permanency.

Gold Hill was on the old road to Auburn from Sacramento, and the placer mines did not prove out as lasting as others, and under the watchful eye of Albert James Gladding, a past master who was Treasurer over an extended period, the Lodge was removed to the more permanent community. Rarely do we mention such a crass matter as commercial companies in connection with Masonry, but as you can surmise, the name of Gladding, when joined with that of McBean, comprises an old and respected firm in California like Gladding McBean and Company, who were in the drainage pipe and tile business when all our great-grandfathers were in those short pants and long stockings we see in old prints.

One of Gold Hill's oldest living postmasters not long ago told me, as I sat under a shade tree at his retirement home in Lincoln-town, that he was the 1913 Master of Gold Hill Lodge. He has lived there most of his life. His name is William Martin Sparks, Jr. He is ninety if he is a day, and was named for Martin Van Buren, the eighth President of the United States. He also told me how to go to Folsom from Lincoln, by car, and I spent several tortuous hours twisting and turning in the foothills trying to find the American River and Folsom over roads that have had but scant travel since our good brother in 1913 held sway among the Masons of Lincoln.

Did you not notice that "junior" after Worshipful Brother Sparks' name and wonder if his father is still living, seeing that he is in his nineties? You know, as I sat talking with the old gentleman I got to wondering about it myself, counting on my fingers, and looking so nonplussed that I wondered that he didn't ask me what was on my mind. So I up and asked. The answer really put me in my place, for the gangling upstart that I am, as he explained it there was really nothing to it at all; any lawyer worth his salt could see it instantly. If he dropped the junior suffix all his papers would have to be changed. Simple when you think of it. Smart people, these past masters of pre-first-world-war days, I only wish we had more of their kind today.

Where was I? Oh, yes, in Lincoln, in the yard of a kindly old gentleman who took me in and gave me a cooling drink on a warm spring day. We fell to talking about Am-Boo, the Chinese gentleman who passed away when our host was a youngster. Had a funeral, a real "Chinee" funeral with paid mourners, a band, and being a Chinese Mason all the Chinese Masons from Sacramento came up and marched in the procession. Made a real impression on Brother Sparks. Who knows, it might have influenced his joining this band of VIP's later in his life. One never knows what it takes to make a lasting impression on a barefoot boy. Banging gongs and all, plus some influential people among the good citizens of Lincoln in the line of march in all truth must have had its impressive way with wide-eyed youth, one William Martin Sparks, Jr.

Not to shorten our story unduly, we did reach Folsom in due course. The restored Mall on Sutter Street gives one about as authentic an impression of the eighteen fifties as anyone could desire, and we discovered and photographed the original Temple where Natoma Lodge No. 64 held forth through many a year when uncertainties and the fluctuation of fortunes and the tide of progress was as best often in the balance.

Both Lincoln and Folsom are at the beginning edge of the slopes of the lowest foothills along the big valley. Neither was in the gold mining districts totally but both were so close that both would, if they could, make pretension to being a part of the gold rush. Of course they both were a part of it, because they were in the "line of fire" of those on their way there. Folsom was right on the American River and hence one cannot say there was no gold to be found in Folsom.

Natoma Lodge No. 65 has certainly come through her pioneering days in great style, for today she has a new plant that can be matched against the best in any part of our great State. Not wishing to offend the weather barons who make preposterous claims for our climate, it could with some justification be stated fairly that Folsom lies in a zone where the temperature soars in the summertime. The new Lodge boasts not one but two air-conditioning plants, one for the Lodge Room proper and one for the Dining and Recreation areas.

But you should see the Lodge Room itself. Not only is it modern in every respect, in design and execution, but retains all that is lovely and respected in the past. By this I mean workmanship. The detailing of the raised portions in the East, West, and South are not passed off as of no particular importance, but are carefully tailored and fine-grain wood paneling and edging is in modest but rich evidence. One immediately knows upon entering the room that here dwell brethren who not only care, but who are eager to put their pocketbooks where many only render advice.

The days when Mormon's Island was the recipient of a Natoma U.D. charter are long since passed away; when Natoma then moved to Folsom, and since that day has flourished as the Bay Tree of the fable. Today she looks eagerly to the future when a growing community needs the lessons Masonry can teach, and Natoma Lodge No. 64 with her rich heritage is in a prime condition to furnish.

The building with the tall iron doors was the Lodge Hall of Natoma No. 64 in Folsom, which was not considered quite a "mother lode" town although it was on the American River where gold was discovered. Sutter's Blacksmith, Samuel Kybers, was a member of this Lodge.

Restored to appear as it did in the Frontier Days, this modern view of the Mall on Sutter Street, Folsom, preserves the flavor of the mid-nineteenth century.

CHAPTER XII

LAND OF THE MIGHTY REDWOOD

HUMBOLDT LODGE NO. 79 and
CRESCENT LODGE NO. 45

Located in downtown Eureka, this is a most impressive building to be located on the northern coast of California; not only does it house a progressive firm, but all the Masonic Bodies of this thriving coastal city, among them Humboldt Lodge No. 79 formed in 1854 in the nearby location of Bucksport. Note the two new shields, or escutcheons, middle of top floor, upon which Masonic emblem is displayed.

In the period of history about which we are writing, many areas of California were set apart. Not from any desire of the inhabitants, but from the facts of nature. California is a country unto itself in size, in variety of landscape, and consequently in the manner of its development. Humboldt County for at least sixty years of its growth has been either handicapped or blessed, depending upon point of view, by being set apart on the northernmost coast with many large and barely passable mountain ranges intervening.

Eureka began, like many another California town, as a place where gold was discovered along the creek-beds. But Humboldt Bay had long been a refuge in storm for the weary sea traveler. However dangerous the bar outside the harbor, it was better than the gales.

Humboldt Lodge No. 79, the first fraternal organization of the region, began its fraternal life in Bucksport, now simply a street area on the fringe of town as one enters from the south.

One is constantly amazed at the number of times the same name will turn up at various Lodges and places, in how many Lodges the same brother has been Master or an active member. For example, H. M. Judah, the captain who commanded troops at Ft. Jones and who was the first Master of North Star Lodge No. 91 at that place, also represented Humboldt Lodge No. 79 at Grand Lodge giving reason why the books and records were delayed, making it possible for a charter to be issued which was done on May 8, 1855. Immediately a hall was erected on a location suitable for a school room on the first floor and the Lodge on the second. We could well surmise that the local Methodist Minister, who also was

This is not a new form of photography but simply two views of one doorway: Humboldt Lodge No. 79 at Eureka. Located at the corner of 5th and G Streets it is one of Eureka's most impressive and better known business centers, the ground floor being devoted to the showrooms of one of America's larger western furniture firms.

In the sweep of redwoods from Richardson's grove to the grove of Jedediah Smith, no finer example of the art of home building will be found nor a better quality of the semper virens be encountered than in the redwood home of our Brother William Carson, in Eureka. Built in 1885 this mansion is still in use, although not in the Carson family. Now a private club, it serves the community of Eureka with elegance and distinction.

county judge as well as a member of the Lodge and a school trustee, had a hand in its early affairs.

From the earliest formation of Lodges in California the problem of enticing sojourning members to join local Lodges has been recognized. Humboldt Lodge tried to cope with this situation, too, in 1855, even though they had by then paid off in full their debt for the Masonic Hall at Bucksport.

Notices were sent to all those in the vicinity of the town of Bucksport to appear for the purpose of affiliating with the Lodge or show cause to the contrary. The notice must have had effect because five new members joined the Lodge. Among them was William Carson, who became one of the most respected members of the community, a founder of one of the northwest's largest lumber empires, and of course, the builder of a famous mansion still to be seen in Eureka.

The following year the first Grand Master to visit Eureka came and spent several days teaching ritual and the lectures of the several degrees. This was none other than William H. Howard, one of the fine names in all the annals of Masonic lore. No sword was available for the tiler but one was obtained from nearby Ft. Humboldt—it is still in the archives of the Lodge to this day.

The Lodge soon moved from Bucksport to Eureka after it became the county seat and the center for growth but not until some excitement over a new temple, and several family squabbles that most all Lodges experience at one time or another, some requiring drastic measures by the supervising higher body, some never quite surviving in vitality and ability to

From 1871 until 1953, a span of 82 years, upon this corner-stone rested the Hall of Crescent Lodge No. 45 near the waves of the rolling Pacific, where in 1896 a tidal wave dislodged the building. Again in 1898 the building was raised from its foundation two feet; in 1964 at time of the Alaska earthquake, it was moved 35 feet. Does anyone know why the carver of this stone engraved "A.F.&A.M." upon it?

carry out the mandates for which all Masons devote their time, their charity and their effort. But on the rock-bound coast of California a sterner breed of men were wont to dwell. Year by year Humboldt Lodge has placed its stamp upon the community of which it is a vital part. Today one of the largest and finest structures of the region is owned and operated by the Masonic Bodies indigenous to the usual large Masonic Temple.

It is located either on or very near the same site upon which the first Eureka located Temple was built. Destroyed by fire in 1867, the Lodge first occupied quarters for which twenty dollars per month was paid.

Lodges such as the one we are discussing, as well as near-by Arcata on Arcata Bay, and further north, Crescent City, were in a position to render much service of emergency nature and of charity beyond the call of the normal Lodge owing to their peculiar location, especially in a day of slow travel and slower communication.

In the month of January 1859, one of the first acts of Masonic charity attributed to Humbolt Lodge, came from a far-away Lodge in San Francisco, Golden Gate No. 30.

Their request had to do with a brother whose life was lost in a wreck resulting from the grounding of the Steamer "Northerner" along the nearby coast. You see, the Indians thereabouts had gathered up the body and buried it, white-man fashion, in a grave. The request from the gentleman's Lodge required his exhumation, identification, and re-burial in accord with ancient custom.

When this old print was made, the automobiles you see were the latest models, and in Eureka, the Masons, as evidenced by Humboldt Lodge No. 79 had really "done themselves proud" with this beautiful edifice that would well grace any city of the land. In Eureka, it was a real bonanza.

Here lies the first Junior Grand Warden. Says Edwin A. Sherman, 33° in Fifty Years of Freemasonry in California, ". . . the oldest chartered Lodge in California, its charter by the Grand Lodge of Missouri being dated May 10, 1848 to Bros. Sachel Woods, W.M., L. E. Stewart, S.W., and Peter Lassen, J.W." Here, after his last illness, where he came from Mexico, Crescent Lodge No. 45, lovingly and dutifully buried him, a last act of Masonic charity. Western Star Lodge No. 2 opened by him at Benton City later was moved to Shasta.

This entranceway to Crescent Lodge No. 45 in their new Temple on 9th Street, Crescent City, is in character with the Northern California Redwood Empire, being made of that material. Its Secretary, Gustave W. Klotz, was Grand Standard Bearer in 1963. Note reflection of a beautiful conifer in the glass pane on the right. An extreme north coastal city, temperature here can almost be counted on in the sixties.

And so the organization grew from small buildings to larger ones, the one occupying the time area from 1870 until about 1924, being most in evidence in earlier books on the history of Freemasonry. The present edifice, whose cornerstone was laid in 1922 under M.W. Grand Master Samuel E. Burke, has proven a wonderful capstone for the excellent growth and stability of Masonry in Humboldt County.

Any Lodge that has the courage to elect a member by affiliation on the evening of December 3, 1857 as this Lodge did, and later in the same evening when it came time to elect officers for the ensuing year, to elect this same brother to the station of Worshipful Master, is a Lodge to be reckoned with. And please pardon the preposition.

Yet, just over a year previously, almost a hundred miles further up the coast of California, brethren of the mystic tie had applied for and received a charter on May 3, 1854, at a place called Crescent City, where Cresecnt Lodge No. 45 came into being. It is now thought by the brethren of this farthest north bay city that their Lodge building was built by the same individual who built the first Masonic Temple in California at Benecia. Crescent City's Lodge has stood sturdily throughout the years until in 1896 a tidal wave of unusual proportions raised the building over two feet. Again in 1898, the hall was dislodged from its cornerstone. In 1925 a great tornado removed part of the building along with its roof. Finally, in 1964 at the time of Alaska's earthquake, a tidal wave of huge proportions moved the building some 35 feet and required its demolition.

No ordinary building was Crescent Lodge No. 45's nor was the Lodge itself just one of ordinary trust and worth. Beautiful in proportion, as is the one at Benecia, and with a floating floor suspended on long beams without supports, it was beloved by the brethren. Just as it was their pride and joy so are they to the smiling rays of approval shining down from the all-seeing eye above them, for here was the Lodge that although in dire straits financially, graciously cared for and paid all the final expenses of a brother whom, although not one of their number, became their duty to assuage and support. It was none other than the first worshipful master of the first Lodge ever to convene in the state of California, and the first elected Junior Grand Warden of this state, who came into their midst as a castaway. After illness had taken its toll in Mexico where he had gone to care for his proper interests, Right Worshipful Brother Saschel Woods arrived in their midst at Gasquet Ranch at the confluence of the Smith river, overcome with a tropical disease. Cared for until his death by this group of brethren of not more than twenty in number, he was tenderly buried in the local cemetery, and a request made upon Grand Lodge to provide suitable marking, which was done.

Today Crescent Lodge No. 45 is the proud possessor of a new and enviable Temple, this time upon higher ground, and is the home of Masons of whose past none need to be ashamed.

CHAPTER XIII

"THE KLAMATH HAD MORE THAN SALMON"

NORTH STAR LODGE NO. 91 and
HOWARD LODGE NO. 37

Over sixty per cent of the first one hundred chartered Lodges have survived fire, flood, dwindling populations, absorption by affiliation and just plain apathy. Among the majority which have lived on is the Lodge at Ft. Jones in Scott's Valley, the Siskiyou County, North Star Lodge No. 91 is fine example of dedication of spirit. Picture above is proof of present intentions.

Coming down off the mountain that scans but does not rival Mt. Shasta, into the Scott Valley, one's spirits are lifted by the sheer beauty of it all. Immediately we think of the early settler who threw in his lot to make a permanent home, and let the gold seekers wander where they would. It is a Claude Monet landscape come to life.

Soon after entering the valley we turn with the river and see in the next mile or two a very tall flagpole, with Old Glory waving a satisfying greeting. What a tall pole for a community that boasts no Air Field or Military Establishment. But this is no ordinary community, this town of Ottitiewa. No, that is not a misspelling; this Indian named locality soon stopped wrestling with the postal authorities just after 1850 or so, and called the town simply Ft. Jones, after the nearby abandoned Army post by that name.

This is the Hall of North Star Lodge No. 91, F. & A. M. on the Main Street of Ft. Jones and whose deed to the part of the building occupied by them (upper story) was dated February 12, 1862 and gave them the "right to build over present building." Only entrance is at rear. A new Temple is now planned for the near future, as this one may be declared unsafe at any time.

Here is a last vestige of Ft. Jones in the Scott Valley of Siskiyou County, many years after its usefulness had been forgotten by the town that grew up a half mile distant. On the Oregon Trail it was a convenient stop-over for travelers.

Instituted a few miles away on the confluence of a gold gulch called by the miners "New York Gulch" where it emptied into Indian Creek, North Star Lodge came into being. This had the Grand Lodge confused, as the first reports said the Lodge was at Indian Creek. The brethren who signed its papers praying for a Dispensation thought they were at a spot called "Hooperville."

Like all mining claims, the population was far from permanent, and by 1861 North Star Lodge No. 91 was moved to Ft. Jones, by now no longer called Ottitiewa. The gold country along the Klamath, and the Scott which drains into it, brought the usual influx of eager miners. After prospecting around for a while, they rushed off to some other place where a report of a rich find circulated.

In those days very little diversion existed; it was difficult to find something to vary the monotony of life. The story is told of the miner who departed to go back east to obtain a bride. In due course he returned, and built a cabin on an eminence near his gold claim. For some reason that the local doctor, Dan Ream, a mainstay of North Star Lodge, could not fathom, he fell sick and died. A proper funeral was given this miner and he was buried at the top of the rise just above his cabin. After the services, the miner's young bride heard a knock at the door, and there stood the parson.

"Madam Melinda," he said, for such was her name, "I am a man of few words. You know that the fair sex are very scarce around these parts, and so I have come to ask you to become my wife."

"Kind sir," replied Melinda, "I very much appreciate your offer, but I am afraid you are just a mite late. You see, the undertaker already asked me at the grave."

In circumstances such as obtained in this far country of mountains and tremendous distances traversed only slowly and painfully by ox-cart and mule-back, when speeding transportation was achieved by swaying concord coach behind four mustang horses, at perhaps ten miles per hour for short periods, it is no wonder that men of like mind, who were Masons in their lives before coming west, banded together to form new Lodges.

One of the best of these, although each has a valid history of its own and no one can be singled out for honors of this kind, was North Star Lodge No. 91. Member Dr. Daniel Ream, of whom we spoke in a light vein, who was an actual personage of this portion of Siskiyou County, lived his life in Ft. Jones and became a legend in his own time. He thought little, we are told, of traveling one hundred and forty miles to care for a sick patient, and for three years, 1859, 1862 and 1863 was Worshipful Master of North Star Lodge. He finally passed away at the ripe old age of 97 and may perpetual light shine upon his soul.

The light of the North Star, shining upon the souls of men, is only the name of one of five such "Stars" that have shined in various parts of the Great Bear's domains. The other four were, first of all, Western Star No. 2 located at Shasta, the very first in the firmament to shine at all. Then there was the Morning Star that sheds its beams upon the far reaches of

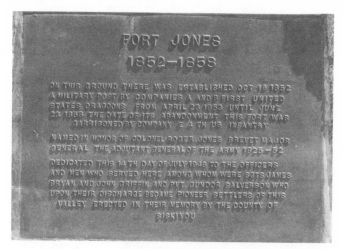

The years 1848 to 1856 were years of tremendous movement and settlement in all the valleys and far reaches of California from border to border and coast to the highest peaks of the Sierra Nevada. To quell the sporadic ravages of the Indians, forts like Ft. Jones were established by the regular Army to support the influx of pioneers from every state of the Union, seeking gold, new homes, and the opportunity to live lives of their own choosing.

Ft. Jones, east of Klamath National Forest, in the County of Siskiyou, the northernmost county of California, is an unusual community. For its size, its spirit and continuity is phenomenal. To this day, its pioneers are numerous and revered. In the above pictures there are at least three early Worshipful Masters and many other names whose descendants have since become members of North Star Lodge No. 91. In 1968 was the seventh Biennial Homecoming celebration of men like those pictured here whose roots were in the old gold fields of Scott Valley in the extreme northwestern portion of the state of California.

53

The Lodge Temple built in 1926 is the home of Howard No. 37 and on or very near this spot has stood the buildings housing both Howard and St. John Lodges in Yreka, Siskiyou County, since the early days. In this Lodge stands a converted grandfather's clock donated by John William Bird (1844-1927) that faithfully carries on the timeless principles of nature's laws as well as the indelible imprint of its donor.

Today, this monument to a bygone era, is all that remains of Ft. Jones, one of the key forts in the northwest. Bro. H. M. Judah, a Captain of the U.S. Army, who rose to be a Major-General of Volunteers in the Civil War, was the first Worshipful Master of nearby North Star Lodge No. 91.

the Great Bay, at Stockton, and it is numbered 68. Then there was Rising Star No. 83 which had its beginning at Forest Hill in the gold area of Placer County, and finally the last star Lodge was Polar Star No. 90 that had its day at the Forks of Poor Man's Creek, in Plumas County under the aegis of none other than Grand Master Willliam H. Howard for whom a Lodge was named that flourished but a few miles from North Star Lodge No. 91 of Ft. Jones.

This North Star Lodge built its home atop another building, as we have seen Sutter Creek do, its second story serving these many years as the home of the dedicated adherents of a way of life familiar to the craft.

And in the County Seat, Yreka, we find the Lodge Hall with not two but with three owners, the Masonic Bodies of all the York Rite holding title to the above floor, and two separate commercial firms holding deeds for the space on the ground floor. There is usually "fireworks" when a bathroom on the upper floor springs a leak.

On North Star's walls are many mementoes of years gone by. One of these, which conveys the idea of the ruggedest individualism and the true spirit of Ft. Jones, is in the form of a letter written to the Grand Master at San Francisco and is dated April 29, 1907. It is headed Hall of "North Star Lodge. No. 91, F. & A.M." and is addressed to Mr. George Johnson, Grand Master, and goes about as follows: "Dear Sir and Brother: Some miserable miscreant has entered our Lodge Room and maliciously destroyed our Charter. Kindly inform us how to proceed in such cases in order that we may get a new Charter for the Lodge, and oblige, Yours Fraternally, Secretary, North Star." Framed, on the same wall, under glass, is the charred remains of the first Charter, a silent reproach to evil-doers, both past and present.

North Star is now contemplating a new home, as the old building shows signs of unrepairable decay. Money to build this new home is now being assembled, and among the sizable contributions is one amounting to four thousand dollars contributed by a "friend of North Star." We mention this transaction because every resident of Ft. Jones undoubtedly knows who the donor is. He is not a member of our Lodge; in fact he is a member of the Roman Catholic Church. He has made no "bones about his reason" for so contributing. It

seems that the local cemetery contains remains of all good Americans, and in its efforts to care for these places of remembrance and sweet sorrow, the Lodge has always done its share of maintenance without "fear or favor," Catholic and Protestant alike, Mason and Profane, all the same. This fact did not go unnoticed.

This is but one sample of the kind of people who make up the town of Ft. Jones, all two hundred or so, of them. Another sample is the Town Museum, open daily, and a credit to the community, illustrating by picture and by artifact its days of glory, and the part it has played in the growth and self-government of a free people.

Even to this writer, an outsider and obviously a "snooper" into its personal affairs, it threw wide its doors of hospitality. Of such are the backbone of America in her hidden grass roots. May her tribe hold fast to all that is good and confound the communists by whatever name called.

Retracing our steps, we returned to the seat of population and County Government, the City of Yreka. There in the gold days ten thousand people gathered to trade, to work, and to live. A dispensation granted on June 12, 1853 gave life to St. John's Lodge that on the succeeding May became St. John's No. 37 and less than three years later, a charter was granted to Howard Lodge No. 96 at the same place, to accommodate the growing number of Masons of Siskiyou County. Side by side these Lodges have flourished, sharing alike not only a Lodge Building but also their very working tools and attending each other's degrees faithfully over the years, until they made a real merger, one dropping its name, the other its number to become one. Thus we have today Howard Lodge No. 37.

And so have the brethren fared in the northern portions of the State. No mention has been made of many great and good men who graced the halls of these retreats of peace and virtue, nor can none be made without fear of lessening these shining examples of how men live and devote their time and talents to a unique influence amidst the toils and cares of the heat of the noonday. Only a complete history can bring them to the fore one by one. Here we must curtail and prune, leaving only the impression that here walked the founders, with the eternal hills, remembered and revered.

For over 100 years this has been the home of North Star Lodge No. 91 and it is one of a very few whose holdings has been built as a second story over an older building. Another is located in Sutter Creek. This hall is the one of few not destroyed by fire over a span of a century and is located in Ft. Jones, Siskiyou County. It, as well as the famous mother lode, is located near "gold country" where the precious metal was assiduously sought, creating many Lodges of temporary stability, as well as many more that flourish to this day. North Star is one of them.

This Lodge on Miner Street, Yreka, Siskiyou County has long been the meeting place for two inseparably intertwined Lodges, St. John's No. 37 and Howard Lodge No. 96. Now they are amalgamated into one Lodge, Howard Lodge No. 37 and it occupies this commercially profitable building in busy Yreka. Like many another, however, this building shares three owners, only the top floor belongs to the Masonic Family of Siskiyou County.

CHAPTER XIV

"NOT ONLY IN TOMBSTONE DID WE SLAP LEATHER"

WESTERN STAR LODGE NO. 2, TRINITY LODGE NO. 27 and VESPER LODGE NO. 84

No Lodge in our jurisdiction perhaps has had as much conversation directed toward it as has this Star of the West Lodge, because it was, according to most historians, the first to bring a charter into California and to open a regular Lodge. This took place at Benton City on October 30, 1849. The Grand Lodge of Missouri had issued the charter on May 10, 1848.

Grand Lodge, through some misinformation concerning dates, awarded the honor of being first to California Lodge No. 1.

However, with true Masonic spirit, and with charity toward her brethren, Western Star Lodge No. 2 has acquitted herself with every good office throughout the years. Benton City, a mining headquarters, like many another, dwindled away and she moved to Shasta, with consent of Grand Lodge and her members, where she was completely burned out at the time the settlement of Shasta burned to the ground. All her property was lost except her Missouri Charter, the charter that named Saschel Woods, L. E. Stewart and Peter Lassen as Master and Wardens.

Her hall was rebuilt in 1853 and from its precincts has issued many brothers who have graced the annals of Masonry throughout the State. From this Temple, now so well preserved and restored that it is pointed out as one of the landmarks of the State Park area of Shasta, have come men of distinction, as well as a Most Worshipful Grand Master, our Brother Clay Webster Taylor.

Probably the oldest Lodge in California, its Charter being dated May 10th, 1848 and issued by the Grand Lodge of Missouri, this is one of the forming Lodges of the Grand Lodge of California. Located at Benton City, later at Shasta, now just about a suburb of Redding, it forms one of a nucleus of buildings of early Shasta County history.

Shasta, the County seat of Shasta County, and the home of Western Star Lodge No. 2, was also the terminus of one of the trails to Oregon. Over parts of this, mail and passenger service continued by means of the above until as late as the middle of the second decade of this century.

At a point about thirty miles above the navigable waters of the central valley's Sacramento River, Shasta became the point of origin for the pack trail to Oregon. First called Reading's Springs, it was County Seat until removed to Redding in 1888. Town burned in 1853 soon after Western Star Lodge No. 2, was moved there from Benton City where it was founded by Saschel Woods and Peter Lassen as the first Lodge of the State of California.

At her Centennial, the Grand Lodge, A.F. & M., of Missouri caused to be erected a bronze plaque in her honor greeting her on the occasion with the expression, "should auld acquaintance be forgot" in honor of the fortitude, courage, and persistence that made an institution from the hopes of three Missouri traveling trappers, explorers and pioneers.

When in this far distant time we speak of pioneers who were the torchbearers of civilization into the Californias, we must not think of them as anything but the tough, deadly-eyed carriers of the lethal weapon of their day, the long-barrel rifle with which they could dot a squirrel's eye at no inconsiderable distance. Ordinarily, the Indian was at their mercy.

One such as these was the first Master of Western Star Lodge. Once while with a large party trading in the west, he took a smaller group of trappers and explorers on a side expedition from Santa Fe to Taos. On their return, taking a short cut on their third day out, they found themselves suddenly surrounded with a very large group of hostile Indians, from whom there was no escape. They were disarmed, taken into the mountains and tied to small trees, around each of which the Indians piled dry brush preparatory to burning, after torture and mutilation. On this occasion it is said that Bro. Woods managed to free his arms, whereupon knowing not what else to do he made certain gestures that no Mason would fail to understand. The Chief immediately freed him, and enlightened him that his party's capture was occasioned by one of them killing a member of his tribe without reason.

Informed that this was untrue, a party was formed to return to Santa Fe to consult with the hotel where Bro. Woods alleged his party slept on the night in question. The truth being corroborated, the whole party had their arms and clothing returned to them and were sent on their way. Soon after this Bro. Woods met Peter Lassen and Western Star Lodge began its labors at Benton City.

A quick glance at a map of northern California will show the geographical relationship between the brethren at Shasta, those at Weaverville, and those just south at Red Bluff. They occupy two sides of a right-angled triangle, the two sides added together being perhaps eighty miles. The reason they form a rough unit is because of the navigability of the mighty Sacramento river up as far as Red Bluff, the home of Vesper Lodge No. 84.

Both Shasta and Red Bluff were terminus points for departure for the Oregon country far to the north. If ever you have traversed a few of the mountain ranges of California, you will understand the reason why we employ the word terminus. Here the mules were loaded, here the crated furniture, the boxes, bales, and impedimenta of every sort were heaved into wagons, and into conestogas, to traverse the beautiful but awesome trails of danger and unknown peril.

Before we leave the water's edge at Red Bluff and see the stern-wheeler turn in the eddying current and head downriver, let us pause to review briefly the history of Vesper Lodge.

In the year 1855, the first Master of Vesper Lodge was

From soon after the Civil War until their last meeting here on January 13, 1967, Trinity Lodge No. 27 met in this Masonic Hall on Main Ctreet, Weaverville, tucked away in the Trinity Alps in the timber and recreation areas of Northern California.

Shasta, a suburb of Redding, California, is the home of Western Star Lodge No. 2, built in 1854, after a disastrous fire destroyed their second home, their first being at Benton City, a mining center, and organized by our first Junior Grand Warden, Saschel Woods, and Peter Lassen, for whom the mountain peak was named. Their California charter was replaced gratis by the Grand Lodge. The original Missouri charter escaped the flames, and is now a prized possession. This building, now a relic for a museum, once was a proud structure among those comprising a flourishing community, pride of the far West.

Brother J. Granville Doll, perhaps a distant cousin of your historian, and in 1955, Vesper in its dedication at its Centennial spoke the following words which are quoted verbatim: "In humble appreciation of the splendid example of our first Grand Master, and those stalwart Brothers who gave Vesper Lodge its beginning, we re-dedicate our lives to the principles of Brotherly Love, Relief and Truth; and with implicit trust in God we rest in the knowledge that the Great Light will shine through future ages and never, never, never die."

Perhaps this will furnish a clue to why these centennial Lodges have survived the years. Vesper is one of them. Burned out of a most sumptuous home on August 16, 1882, they rebuilt. In December of 1924 again the Lodge, located at the corner of Main and Oak Streets, lost its hall by fire. This location, occupied since 1871, was just a stone's throw from the landing wharf where the side-wheelers unloaded their cargoes.

Today Vesper Lodge No. 84 has become a prosperous and active group of brothers whose illustrious past inspires them to carry on the traditions leading to a worthy and well-deserved future.

As we leave the river at Red Bluff, imagine you are with a wagon train bound for Weaverville, the latest gold diggings, in the Trinity "Alps" and the year is 1853. In the train is 985 pounds of freight for Trinity Masonic Lodge No. 27 for which the brethren at Weaverville paid 2¼ cents per pound to have it brought from San Francisco, or just over twenty-two dollars. It could well be the beautifully carved chairs for the

This obelisk to Peter Lassen, first Junior Warden of Western Star No. 2 is located near Honey Lake in Eastern Lassen County, and a Lodge at Susanville is named for this early Danish pioneer to California. He was the owner of Rancho Bosquejo in what is now Tehama County, helping to hold together the early home of Western Star at Benton City before it moved to Shasta.

This is the new modern plant of Trinity Lodge No. 27 at Weaverville into which the Lodge recently moved after the many years of climbing the circular staircase on the principal thoroughfare. Here tradition lives anew and speaks with modern voices to a new generation of Masons who will carry forward the time-honored principles of truth and justice.

Up this winding staircase, until just a few years ago, trod the feet of the great and the near-great to attend Trinity Lodge No. 27 which for over a century carried on the traditions of stalwarts like Wiley James Tinnen, William Spencer Lowden, John C. Burch, Dr. William Ware, John Carr and Arthur Paulsen all of whom have been mighty proponents of advancing civilization in this wooded region of northwest America.

Under extremely difficult lighting conditions, this copy of an old print was taken because of the importance of its subject, one which few Masons can claim complete forgetfulness. Rarely do we see them, together, as represented here. This litho is one of the highly prized treasures of Trinity Lodge No. 27, at Weaverville, Trinity County, in the northern, smog-free, pine clad portion of the great Bear State of California.

three principal officers' stations, for, as the present Secretary says, "they were carried on floats to Red Bluff, and thence by land to Weaverville." He has a point.

Trinity Lodge being necessarily of the "purist" type, by which we mean that being here in Weaverville, a County Seat that even yet has no traffic light nor parking meter in all its miles and miles of lakes and forest, the Lodge has every opportunity to study its ritual and realize a perfection that others, more distracted, never achieve. At any rate, it has furnished our State of California with two Grand Masters, first, in 1885 Most Worshipful Wiley J. Tinnin, a Trinity County Superior Court Judge, and in 1950 another distinguished jurist, Most Worshipful Brother Charles Arthur Paulsen, who today lives in retirement with his wife in Weaverville.

No account, however brief, can omit the name of William S. Lowden, who is said by our Masonic historian, Leon O. Whitsell, to be the "toughest thing that ever sat astride horseflesh." In 1853 when Adams Express and Wells Fargo battled it out for supremacy by racing to deliver the President's message, Brother Bill Lowden received the relay at Tehama, and covered the intervening sixty miles in two hours and thirty-seven minutes. Changing horses nineteen times, he arrived in Shasta just in time to find that his relief man could not continue to Weaverville. So Lowden continued the additional forty miles, and incidentally by now it was snowing lightly, and such mountains you have never seen, arriving in Weaverville two hours and thirty-six minutes later. Once, when robbers held up a stagecoach for $31,000 he chased the highwaymen all over the northern mountains and with a deputy from Butte County finally finished off the looters at Marysville, where he had to put the deputy, poor fellow, to

This chart, or Master's Carpet, one of three, is very early and shows Bro. Lafayette—in the oval left of Washington —with inscription, "An Order Whose Leading Star is Philanthropy." The oval on the right is of Dr. Joseph Warren, and the inscription says, "M.W. Grand Master for the Continent of America 1772-9." These charts are framed and hung in the South, West, and East of Trinity Lodge No. 27, Weaverville, California.

Framed behind glass, this Masonic Apron, apparently was made from unbleached muslin or from linen, and bears the date 1776 placed there by the framers. However, we note it is a square apron, not round as worn by Geo. Washington. Interesting questions arise from the nature and shapes of these old aprons. This one may have been "squared" by the picture-framer.

bed to recover.

Yet Lowden lived to construct a mountain road between Buckhorn Valley and Weaverville, a distance of twenty-five miles, that is yet today a model of roadbuilding, a marvel to engineers because he constructed it for less than $30,000 over two mountain ridges. This, in 1857 when a dollar was a dollar.

We have mentioned our historian who wrote "One Hundred Years of Freemasonry in California," a work every Mason owes it to himself to read. I cannot, however, but pass on to you a story, authentic yet humorous that relates to our Grand Master Whitsell, who was vastly interested in early Masonic pioneers.

Once, we are told, he learned of a certain brother in his early nineties, who lived at Milpitas just outside San Jose. He arranged to visit him in advance, arrived on the appointed day, and was conducted by his daughter, a middle-aged lady, to the back kitchen. There, in an old rocker sat the elderly brother, long white beard and all. As the interview proceeded, the old gentleman would pause, and address himself to a can placed approximately six feet away in the center of the room. His aim was deadly. This continued throughout the afternoon, and upon leaving as he stepped outside the front door, the daughter who accompanied him said, "Mr. Whitsell, I want to apologize to you for the actions of my father. You know he never chewed tobacco in his life, but the last month preparing for your arrival, he did not want to disappoint your image of him, so each day he practiced and had me move that can just one inch farther away, until he reached the limit of his ability."

Even Trinity Lodge No. 27 would be hard put to top that.

A careful observation at the bottom, left, of the unfinished Temple, will reveal a procession with body-bearers returning for more decent interment. All the lessons of the third degree are portrayed, with the center depicting that of lasting importance, the whole overshadowed by the all-seeing eye. Note the clothing of Father time and the absence of other raiment.

The Fellow Craft represents a man laboring in the pursuit of truth; and the Winding Stairs are the devious pathways of that pursuit. Here is an old legend seldom mentioned or accounted for; here the trivium and quadrivium of the seventh century hold sway; here the sacred number fifteen is totaled and the secret laws of nature revealed.

In the middle 1850s this pastoral and somewhat idyllic scene, taken within 100 yards of the main street of downtown Red Bluff, shows the Sacramento River at the end of navigation, where the river steamers like the River Steamer (sternwheeler) Dover and Chrysopolis tied up at the Red Bluff terminus. There began the long trek by wagon and horseback to Oregon and waypoints like Weaverville and Shasta.

Vesper Lodge No. 84, located at 822 Main Street in Red Bluff, is the culmination of her many homes throughout her long history, and is a living monument to those brethren who never say die in the face of adversity. Located on one of the valuable pieces of real estate in the city of Red Bluff its future seems assured.

Any investigator, antiquarian, or historian or whatever who begins to delve into early times, will soon find a maze of crisscrossing claims. Here is a restored wall of Shasta County Court House. The town of Shasta was burned in 1853, along with its Masonic Hall. (Western Star No. 2). Another adobe dwelling is also reputed to be a "First Court House Shasta County 1851." At this far date it means to us that life in the 1850s was fluid, fast-moving, and of a rugged nature.

These sternwheelers are tied up along the upper reaches of the Sacramento River at what is now believed to be the west bank of the river at Red Bluff.

Cargo and passenger carrying vessels of this type brought supplies, furniture and personnel for the pack trains and wagon trips into the wilderness to the north, however wild and beautiful. Here came the beautifully carved chairs occupying the stations of Lodges like Trinity No. 27 at Weaverville.

This authentice adobe may well have been the first Court House in Shasta County. However, the building erected in 1855, four years later than the caption on this 'dobe, may also have housed the early seat of law and order.

No text accompanied this old print, obtained through the courtesy of an old and respected photographic firm of Red Bluff, and we are sure if it could speak for itself, many tales of early desperadoes would hold us spellbound.

CHAPTER XV

"THEREFORE FAINT NOT, NOR BE WEARY IN WELL-DOING"

YOLO LODGE NO. 81   SUISUN LODGE NO. 55

The more one reflects upon the life histories of Lodges like Yolo and Suisun, the more respect one feels for them. For they are of that number of small Lodges that survived through all the vicissitudes of time and circumstance which kill off lesser breeds of men.

Both of these Lodges were burned out of their fraternal homes, not once but several times. Yolo has always been a group that has striven for community betterment and their first built Lodge, their second home, occupied the second floor of a building providing the first floor for public school purposes. Although records are slim, in 1874 land was purchased and with the help of Cacheville School District a building was provided that was the finest in that part of Yolo County. This building lasted thirty-three years when it was taken by fire. Some of the early schooling of Most Worshipful Grand Master William H. Fisher was received by him in this building.

Once again the Lodge and the School District pooled resources and erected another school and Masonic Hall whose cornerstone was laid by Grand Master George M. Perine on July 27, 1908 and completed that same year. In this building their seventy-fifth anniversary was celebrated and the guest of honor was Grand Master Charles M. Wollenberg.

And then a few years later, in 1946 their Hall burned again. This time assistance from the brethren state-wide poured in; in fact, from more than four hundred and forty active Lodges came funds to assist these brethren of Yolo Lodge No. 81 to finance their fourth Masonic home. The cornerstone of the Lodge today was laid June 7, 1947 by Past Grand Master Leslie E. Wood, their first meeting being held in October. Yolo Lodge again is on its way.

Both of these names, Yolo and Suisun, are derived from the original Indian inhabitants of the region, and incidentally, the latter is pronounced "Sue-Soon," the third letter being

Time deals kindly with some communities; but not with Yolo. Early it was the County Seat of Yolo County, today the seat of government has long since removed to Woodlands, nine miles closer to Sacramento, and a larger center. In the midst of rich agricultural lands, Yolo, now dropped from the maps, bravely carries on in this 1947-built Lodge Hall where no less than eighteen sons of members have followed their fathers into Masonic Membership in the Lodge called Yolo No. 81.

This residence in Yolo undoubtedly was the early home of Yolo Lodge No. 81. One of its oldest members, Jim Cleary, once owned it and verifies the raised ledge around the principal room upstairs. This plus the old cash book stating the old Lodge was purchased for $150 and moved to a lot owned by Judge Hutton for remodelling, is the final link of apparent proof, as the house here is on that portion of the Hutton estate to which it was removed.

silent. Suisun is located at the head of the Bay after which it is named, but of late years the road mappers tend to call it Grizzly Bay. It is at the beginning of a great sweep of grasslands and rich agricultural region divided into the two Counties of Solano and Yolo. Yolo originally was called Cochran's Crossing and is located on Cache Creek. It is in the middle of a vast valley of rich producing lands over which no longer the antelope, the deer and wild Mexican horses roam, but now the snorting spouts of the tractors pull the gang plows by the dozen.

Both Yolo and Suisun represent the culmination of a century and more of steady growth and effort of those men of the soil, of the home, of the professions, who devote their lives to the support of moral underpinning of every grassroot community in America. Yolo is proud of its second, third and even fourth generation of sons who carry on a proud tradition. Suisun has weathered the storms and the changes of circumstances and now is engaged in a building program that is second to none in the State of California.

The hand of friendship is extended to these true brothers.

This mellow building is still basking in its aura of former splendor and is the present home of Suisun Lodge No. 55 which will soon change its habitat to a modern home some two miles distant. This thoroughly Masonic structure located on the main street of the fast disappearing town of "Suisun City" is now no longer shown on maps, having been absorbed by nearby Fairfield. The town nestles at the head of the marshy formerly Suisun Bay now called Grizzly Bay.

This modern structure erected by the members of Suisun Lodge No. 55 is located in a fast growing area of Fairfield, the County Seat of Solano County, rich agriculture region, thirty-five miles southwest of Yolo and Woodland. Costing something under two hundred thousand dollars when completed and occupied, these brethren have been able to "pay as you go" a feature that will save thousands of dollars in interest charges in the years to come.

CHAPTER XVI

"THE STURDY OAK OF ALAMEDA COUNTY"

LIVE OAK LODGE NO. 61

"How Sturdy An Oak" may grow from a small acorn may be ascertained from this Oakland Masonic Memorial Temple located at 3903 Broadway. The land it occupies is valued at more than a quarter of a million dollars, and the edifice erected upon it represents better than a million and a quarter, approaching a total of nearly one and three-quarter million dollars. "The small acorn" is represented by a building owned by Edson Adams at the foot of this same Broadway near the wharf, in 1854, over a carriage shop valued a skimpy thousand or two.

It seems to me presumptuous that anyone but a native born son of Oakland should write of the birth, growth, and flourishing strength of Live Oak Lodge No. 61. Surely this condensation of their magnificent history can but sadden rather than gladden the hearts of those lives that are twined about her altars. Yet the past can speak through the heart and soul that connects us all like a gold thread which forever will inspire us—through the Fatherhood of God and the Brotherhood of man. It unites us in a way every brother is bound to understand.

Oakland was but four years old when a few Masons realized they needed to band together to live their lives in harmony and usefulness, and so on a Friday evening in August of 1854 they met for the first time, to plant a little acorn that has grown into a mighty oak.

In due course a charter was issued: the acorn had sent down a tender feeler-root. Times were lush, the outpouring of humanity from, it seemed, every quarter of the globe had come to taste the riches of Ophir. Yet, three years later, a great recession developed· partly as a result of too zealous use of the hydraulic placer mining method, partly because many who came did not find the riches they envisioned, until a wave of public frustration developed along with closing of banks and a general feeling of hopelessness.

The little acorn felt this, too, and reduced her rent of her hall from fifteen dollars downward. On one fateful night, the night before the fourth of July, 1857, a resolution was offered that Live Oak Lodge No. 61 deliver up her Charter to Grand Lodge, succumbing to lack of interest and the downward trend of the times. On August 7 the measure was defeated

The inside of this modern structure must be "seen to be believed," it is that fine. If one desired to be selective without deserting the bounds of good taste, being desirous of but emulating that noble contention, or rather emulation of who best can work and best agree, we would select this group of brethren. Through all the one hundred fourteen years of their Masonic life they typify being among the best our craft can offer both in moral and material excellence.

after one of the finest rallies to the defense of Masonry one could wish to hear. The brother who rallied the Lodge pointed out that "Masonic Lodges differ from every other organization, in that they have only one way of growth. No one is ever solicited and not everyone who knocks upon the door is admitted to membership. The Initiate who comes seeking 'Light' has seen that 'Light' in us. We cannot plead the poverty of the times as the reason for our situation. A long history reveals that Masonry has shown its greatest vigor during periods of adversity. During the Colonial period, when the economic situation could scarcely have been worse, there was a constant and solid growth of the Fraternity."

This brother who rallied the Lodge to new endeavor was Francis Kittridge Shattuck. He asked those present to rededicate themselves to the practice of those virtues which the Order teaches. The membership at this point had dwindled to sixteen. This boost to their morale electrified them and the Lodge paid off its indebtedness and began to grow. By 1859 the little acorn had taken root. In 1860 when the first rider of the Pony Express reached San Francisco carrying the mail, Live Oak had reached a membership of 35.

And so the seedling oak began to grow. Ten years or so later it had passed the one hundred mark in membership. Not that problems did not exist, nor growing pains were less than many another fledgling Lodge. Yet something indefinable and

This is the corner of Twelfth and Washington Streets in Oakland, the modernized version of the Masonic Temple and home of Live Oak Lodge No. 16 from its dedication in 1883 until 1966. This viewing was probably made in the middle thirties, so says the long skirts and the parked automobile.

This Masonic Temple, Home of Live Oak Lodge No. 61 until recently, was dedicated Feb. 22, 1881 and was not destroyed by the earthquake of 1906 although adjacent buildings lost some of their walls. It was opened as a refugee center. Compare this rendition with the modernization which took place after 1906. Roofline altered, gingerbread, towers gone, the only clue is the window-wells. (Modernization date was 1933.) This is the corner of Twelfth and Washington Streets, Oakland.

difficult to put one's finger on began to become apparent. It is an éclat, an élan, an esprit de corps, call it what you will, that grows in a certain climate of fellowship and brotherly love that defies definition or exact interpretation, yet one can sense and feel it, not only in assemblages of brethren, but in the buildings themselves which they constantly inhabit.

This indefinable something began to grow and nourish the Live Oak, until finally it became a sturdy young hardwood able to withstand the stronger storms. One of these was the occurrence, now world-famous, when at at 5:13 a.m. on the morning of the 18th of April, 1906, the city of San Francisco suffered an earthquake. Not that Oakland across the bay did not feel this earthquake, it did, even the building, next door to the now sumptuous brick and stone Temple at Twelfth and Washington Streets, suffered, losing its front wall which fell into the street.

While the fires of San Francisco raged, Worshipful Master W. S. Smith of Live Oak Lodge along with the Most Worshipful Grand Master Motley H. Flint threw open the doors of the Temple to refugees by the hundreds, while food and clothing was gathered and sent transbay to the destitute there. In the minutes we find the following, ". . . owing to the damaged condition of the Temple and the upset condition of society in general no degree work for the month of May will be held."

This is Twelfth Street, Oakland, looking west from Broadway, and there, just this side of the Church, is the famous Masonic Temple that underwent such a transformation from this picture in 1884 to the one in the middle 1930s shown in another picture. The horse in the lower right is about to make a fast delivery—provided his master comes and awakens him from his daily meditations.

These gentlemen are the Officers of Live Oak Lodge No. 61 of Oakland for the Year 1894. It is hoped that the reader can devote about fifteen seconds to the face of each brother, for each is a man of substance and character and well worth the scrutiny. The Junior Warden is on the Master's right, Senior Warden, left. The Tiler is the one *with the long full beard. The Chaplain is on the extreme left, the Marshal, extreme right. Names, in the year 1968 are probably unnecessary. What, however, is the shaggy dog, on which the Master's feet rest, and what is the Junior Warden holding?*

Relief funds totaling more than $315,000 were received from all parts of the United States, Canada, Mexico, Ireland, South Australia and Hungary by the Relief Bureau of Grand Lodge. The work was carried out efficiently and was a task ably performed. Masonry met the emergency.

By 1907 there were 638 members in Live Oak Lodge and the city of Oakland had passed the 125,000 mark. The oak was maturing at a lively rate.

It is a practical impossibility to enumerate in a brief skit of this nature all the personages, both great and small, who have passed the doors of this outstanding exemplification of the Masonic Craft. Let it suffice to say that every public office has had its share and felt the influence of its members: mayors, aldermen, councilmen, congressmen, lawyers, doctors, commercial entrepreneurs of every stripe have known the fellowship of this Lodge. Being close to the Masonic Home, it has played a part in its development; being in the thick of affairs around the Great Bay on whose shores it has taken root, it furthered the 1939 Golden Gate International Exposition by fostering a turnout of 20,000 Masons and their family into Treasure Island on "Masonic Day." By 1940 the federal census showed the Great Bear State as fifth in the Union with over six million inhabitants, while Oakland had grown to 350,000 and the Sturdy Oak displayed over nine hundred on its rolls.

As the Centennial for this early Lodge approached, its officers conceived a very wonderful idea for a centennial gift to the Lodge itself. They should have a new set of officer's jewels cast from solid gold. And so the call went forth. You should have seen the response, in the form of more than 2,000 pieces of gold consisting of watches, rings, chains, pins, yes, even one gold toothpick, went into the formation of these 14-carat works of art. The Golden Jewels of Live Oak Lodge will live on to grace the branches of the towering Oak of Oakland.

Twelve years have come and gone since the Centennial celebration and the Oak has again increased in strength and stability, for on May 7, 1966 was dedicated a new home for Live Oak Lodge, undoubtedly one of the finest in all the broad land of the USA. Here, among the finest traditions any Masonic organization could wish for, will be carried forward into the future the tenets of Brotherly Love, Relief, and Truth. Here, the shining objects of art cherished through the years will find a home that sets them off to perfection. Here, the Pillars of the Porch, the most massive certainly and among the most impressive of any in the land, have found themselves at rest. Here, the spirits of those sturdy pioneers who braved the dangers of a continent will at last come to repose, smiling benignly down upon those neophytes who now tremulously approach to answer the ever old yet ever new query as to who approaches our sacred portals.

As we reminisce that the sturdy oak was not to become strong after its hopeful germination in the summer of 1854 without exposure to the elements, so Arthur R. Andersen, historian for this Lodge, has said, and we shall turn to him for a fitting benediction to this saga of American Freemasonry: "It was to know the warm sunshine of Faith and Brotherly Love, the nurturing showers of Devotion and Fidelity, as well as the harsh winds of Discouragement and Indifference; and, as the Nation passed through all the phases of its development, in changes in transportation, in communication, in manufacturing, the extension of public education, the recognition of human rights, emerging from each phase stronger in spiritual and material resources; so also do we see Live Oak Lodge No. 61 come to its one hundredth birthday as the enduring Symbol of a great Fraternity of Free Men, who bend the knee to God alone."

And by this example shall we all profit—or perish.

It is no wonder it was named Live Oak Lodge when the live oak trees grew right in the middle of the street. Incidentally, the building on the left above the trees is Dr. Durant's School which later became the University of California. This is 1869, the year the first through train came in from the east. You are on the corner of Broadway, Oakland, looking down Twelfth Street.

On May 10, 1869 at Ogden, Utah the two men with silver
hammers drove the last spikes of gold and silver joining
the east and west, and on November 8, 1869 the first
transcontinental train, above, pulled into Oakland, California. The Engine is Central Pacific's No. 116. The train
was greeted by a royal welcome by citizens of Oakland not
to mention Live Oak Lodge members whose Lodge then
was just fifteen years old.

This "king-size" Past Master's Jewel could
well have belonged to any of our early
Lodges. It was the custom to utilize the
large size jewel, and this specimen is typical of those worn during the last half of
the nineteenth century.

These remarkable Pillars, in Live Oak Lodge No. 61 in Oakland,
have 1885 stamped on the inside, each globe is said to weigh 198
lbs., and beside being "huge" both in height and girth, they are
the most beautiful we have seen. This is the Lodge that is more
than 100 years old. Can you read the inscription over the doorway that appears to be arabic?

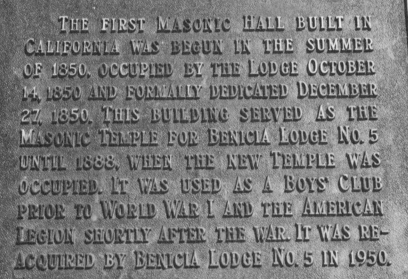

FIRST MASONIC HALL
BUILT IN CALIFORNIA

THE FIRST MASONIC HALL BUILT IN
CALIFORNIA WAS BEGUN IN THE SUMMER
OF 1850, OCCUPIED BY THE LODGE OCTOBER
14, 1850 AND FORMALLY DEDICATED DECEMBER
27, 1850. THIS BUILDING SERVED AS THE
MASONIC TEMPLE FOR BENICIA LODGE NO. 5
UNTIL 1888, WHEN THE NEW TEMPLE WAS
OCCUPIED. IT WAS USED AS A BOYS' CLUB
PRIOR TO WORLD WAR I AND THE AMERICAN
LEGION SHORTLY AFTER THE WAR. IT WAS RE-
ACQUIRED BY BENICIA LODGE NO. 5 IN 1950.

ERECTED BY THE HISTORIC LANDMARK
COMMITTEE, NATIVE SONS OF THE GOLDEN WEST,
BENICIA PARLOR NO. 89 NATIVE SONS OF THE
GOLDEN WEST AND BENICIA PARLOR NO. 287
NATIVE DAUGHTERS OF THE GOLDEN WEST,
MARKER DEDICATED ON DECEMBER 17, 1950.

CALIFORNIA HISTORICAL LANDMARK
REGISTRATION NO. 174.

*Along with 726 Montgomery Street, San Francisco, where
California Lodge No. 1 held their first meeting, and at
Shasta, in Shasta County where Western Star No. 2 holds
an early Charter, here Benicia Lodge No. 5 joins the early
ones with the first Masonic Temple built in California.
Owned by Benicia today and still in use as a historic spot
for conferrals of degrees, its many artefacts preserves the
flavor of pioneer times.*

CHAPTER XVII

"WHEREVER MASONS MET LODGES WERE BUILT"

MARTINEZ LODGE NO. 41,
BENICIA LODGE NO. 5 and
NAVAL LODGE NO. 87

While many towns around the San Francisco Bay Region have names that are of Spanish origin, none perhaps can surpass Martinez for a colorful and interesting past.

Situated on the Carquinez Straits which connect San Pablo Bay—San Pablo Bay is the northern bulge on your map— with what was once called Suisun̄ Bay but now on some references is called Grizzly Bay, Martinez, since the familiar date of 1776, did continue, up to the discovery of gold, a strictly Mexican and native Californian settlement. It boasted a marvelous climate, fertile soil and is among beautiful rolling hills. No wonder that in 1848 Robert Semple came over from San Francisco, took a liking to it and made something of a splash.

Not literally, of course, but one of the things he did was to establish a ferry across the treacherous, if narrow, straits between Martinez and Benicia. Robert Semple was a Freemason. He also was a dentist, as well as the proverbial one-man chamber of commerce. As the goldrush developed, this ferry became an important link in the movement of men from San Francisco to the goldfields. And so Martinez began to grow. Soon there were sufficient Masons to form a Lodge, the first meeting place being in a typical Monterey-type adobe belonging to one José Santos Berryessa, who shortly petitioned the Lodge and became the first Mason to be raised in Martinez Lodge No. 41. Not a little coincidental that the first was born in California, and that he was among the very few at this early time when lines of cleavage to a certain religion were very strong and very nearly universal in this part of the world.

The first master of Martinez Lodge No. 41 was Right Worshipful Brother N. W. Wood who simultaneously was Junior Grand Warden under Grand Master William H. Howard. The first Worshipful Master, as did many another Mason in the early days of settling California, later applied for and received a demit. In 1857 while engaged in an enterprise that undoubtedly has some political overtones, he found himself as far south as the present State of Sonora in Mexico proper. On a certain morning in June he, along with a companion, were victims of a Mexican firing squad. Unsettled times in the year 1857 made many causes unpopular, and some dangerous to life and limb.

It is interesting that Martinez Lodge shows that its original by-laws are titled not F. & A.M. but F. & A.A.Y.M. which is, of course, the Southern custom for Free and Accepted Ancient York Masons. This year, 1857, was also the year a new Temple was constructed, and the deed called for property in the names of the Master and Wardens of Martinez Lodge No. 41, F. & A.A.Y.M.

Almost repetitiously throughout this book, we have mentioned the fact that times and circumstances in early gold days of California were fluid and fast-moving. Martinez was no exception, it too being in the full stream of passing humanity to and from the gold diggings. It had its share of trials and errors and rough going. One in particular that is mentioned by Most Worshipful Brother Whitsell, our 100-year historian, relates to a brother who was tried by a Masonic trial, found guilty and expelled. But twelve years later he was back, petitioned for reinstatement on the grounds that he had been innocent. His story was believed and on ballot was restored to full membership, lived a creditable life, and was accorded Masonic honors upon his death, and expressions of sorrow were published and furnished his widow.

Just this brief look into the affairs of Martinez Lodge should indicate clearly that here is a typical pioneer Masonic Lodge, with a colorful and impressive history that few Lodges can equal. The time has come, as much as we would like to continue, to cross the narrow neck of water to Benicia, where an earlier Lodge flourishes, one that also, like Martinez, traces its origin to the Southern dominions, and early offered its support and assistance to the brethren of Martinez.

In fact, Dr. Robert Semple, said to be a man seven feet tall, took a shine to Benicia's location, and with Thomas O. Larkin founded the town right after the Bear Flag trouble in 1846. Having brought General Vallego as a prisoner to Sacramento, he learned the land belonged to him, purchased it from him and laid out the town of Benicia calling it Francisca after General Vallejo's wife.

At any rate, calling the town Francisca so incensed the town fathers of San Francisco that they changed its name from the then name of Yerba Buena. This of course preempted the name of San Francisco, and Semple and Larkin called theirs Benicia, another name of General Vallejo's wife.

This is the corner of Thompson and Estudillo Streets, in Martinez, one of the old Spanish-Mexican towns on San Francisco Bay where Martinez Lodge No. 41 took its rise. In Martinez was the home of John Muir, famous naturalist, and one of the legendary figures of Yosemite. A lively dispute rages as to whether or not he was a Freemason, but there are no records in Martinez Lodge to substantiate this.

Old Benicia Temple, built in the summer of 1850, occupied by Benicia Lodge No. 5 in October, stands today sturdy and strong and now again owned by the Lodge. Like Columbia Lodge, it is open to be used in conferring degrees; incidentally, such degrees do not require dispensation, as its Charter so stipulates, and its Junior Warden will make arrangements for refreshments.

This "friendly" rivalry between Yerba Buena and Francisca, excuse me, I mean between San Francisco and Benicia, as we must now call them, continued. Benicia secured the first protestant communion in the State, and one of the first hotels of consequence. It also secured the United States Arsenal, as well as U.S. Army Headquarters for California.

So it is no wonder that Benicia Masons erected the first official Masonic Temple, still standing and in constant use, and again owned by Benicia Lodge, as it passed from their hands after 1888 when their "new" or second Temple was built.

Dr. Semple, first Master of Martinez, Judge in Contra Costa County, president of the State Constitutional Convention held in Monterrey, member of the Bear Flag Party, was Charter Treasurer of Benicia Lodge. Benjamin D. Hyam, first Master of Benicia Lodge, became the third Grand Master of the Grand Lodge of California. There is no desire on the part of this observer to engage in the difficult role of separating the skein of tangled threads that constitute the formation of Grand Lodge, or in evaluating the priority of which Lodge was first in California. But Brother Ben Hyam was no novice at parliamentary procedure, Southern gentleman that he was. When the Grand Lodge formed he was there, but in his pocket was no Dispensation for Benicia. Had there been, it must have been rejected for at that moment no one knew that the Grand Lodge differences in Louisiana under which such a Dispensation for formation had been issued were healed. But as a simple delegate from his Lodge at Benicia, he could be accepted, and was.

Another name on the Charter of Benicia Lodge that is familiar to you is that of Sachel Woods. It was he who was designated by the Grand Master to come to Benicia and install its first Charter Officers.

A visit to Benicia Lodge is worthwhile. Many artifacts will interest even the casual Mason. The whale oil lamps, used before the discovery of kerosene, are there. Candlelight

Benicia Lodge No. 5 built this "new" Temple in 1888. Because of fires, floods, tidal waves, and the obsolescence of time, many Lodges of our jurisdiction are holding out in structures no newer than this one, at the corner of 106 West "J" Street in Benicia. The spire of the church on the left is probably also approaching 100 years of continuous service. Benicia is a historic spot on Carquinez Straights in the East Bay portion of San Francisco Bay.

also played its part, and there are candlesticks that came around the horn by sailing vessel, cast from iron and weighing fifty pounds apiece. There are original chairs over one hundred years now in use. The Bible was donated by Brother Thomas Stanley, a founding member, and was the ship's bible of the sailing ship, U.S.S. SAVANNAH, a frigate, which happened to be anchored near Benicia during the founding of the Lodge. The pillars are plain but very old and were used in the mine fields by Nevada Lodge No. 13 and by Quitman Lodge No. 88, before its consolidation with Nevada.

Benicia Lodge welcomes visitations from other Lodges to its historic Temple in order that others may come and share in its history.

The third city around the perimeter of the Bay Area is Vallejo, just opposite Mare Island. This North Bay location is but a short distance from Benicia, and is the home of Naval Lodge No. 87. It is one of the largest Lodges of the jurisdiction and along with Live Oak No. 61 and San Diego No. 35 is characterized by that indefinable something which gives a Lodge a special spirit and standing among its fellows that is much more than its size alone.

Most Worshipful Brother Henry C. Clausen, 33°, who was Grand Master when Naval Lodge celebrated its one hundredth anniversary in 1955, said in his letter of incorporation into their prepared booklet in honor of that occasion that it should ever be remembered that Masonry has been an important thread in the fabric of our State's unparalleled growth in the last century. He also indicated that the best part was yet to come, in its growth and usefulness.

Situated opposite the Naval Station and Navy Yard for more than the one hundred years, the basic pattern of Naval Lodge has been the artisans and Mare Island workers, as well as a group drawn from Naval personnel themselves. Here is a perfect meshing of the symbols of Masonry and the operative crafts of every description with which its members are daily engaged. The yard was first put into operation on Sep-

tember 16, 1854 under Commander Farragut who later became the famous Admiral of the Civil War days.

While the stability and success of the Nation's Naval prowess undoubtedly can be traced to the influence of this nearby Lodge of Masons, we must not overlook the aphorism that many institutions are the lengthened shadow of but one man. While here it is the lengthened shadow of many acting in concert, we do have in Naval Lodge No. 87 the rise of one of the greats of our American history, John Mills Browne (1831-1894).

Brother Browne just briefly graduated from Harvard University Medical Department in 1852, became a Naval Surgeon, served aboard the U.S.S. Kearsarge during the Civil War and went on to become the Surgeon General of the U.S. Army. He is buried in Arlington.

But the part of his life most concerned with Naval Lodge is the fact that while at Mare Island he affiliated with the Lodge and became its Master in 1871. The same year he was elected Junior Grand Warden and became our Fifteenth Grand Master serving successively in 1875, 1876, 1877 and 1878. He was a York Rite Mason serving in the Grand Chapter, Royal Arch Masons of California and received his thirty-third degree in the Scottish Rite from the hands of the late great Albert Pike, 33°, and in 1886 was elected Treasurer-General of the Supreme Council for the Southern Jurisdiction of the United States.

There is a delightful custom in this Naval Lodge No. 87 wherein the beautiful past master's jewel belonging to Brother Browne is installed in a brief ceremony around the neck of each outgoing master. The jewel was presented to the Lodge by the widow of Dr. Browne, who herself was the granddaughter of the author of "The Star Spangled Banner," the immortal Francis Scott Key.

Breathes there a man with soul so dead that never to himself has said, this is my own, my native land?

Benicia, named for the wife of General Mariano Guadalupe Vallejo, last Governor of California under Mexico, was the third State Capitol of California after it became a State of the Union. The above building housed the State Legislature in 1853-54 and is still standing. Benicia currently is a small city located east of San Pablo Bay on Carquinez Straight, it was early an important center for boat building and development of the Bay Area.

What is so special about 707 Marin Street, Vallejo? For one thing it shows the permanence of the detail and good construction that even in a war-time year (1917) was prevalent. And it shows from the worn marble where countless feet have trod, that Masonry plays a heavier part in the affairs of a community and in the U.S. Navy than one sometimes suspects.

The corner of Marin and Virginia Streets in Vallejo has been the home of the Masonic Order in that East Bay city for more than a hundred years. This structure, built in 1917, replaced one built in 1866. Before this the Naval Lodge occupied the old "Aspenall Building," a poorly ventilated box-like building, at the northeast corner of Virginia and Santa Clara Streets called the "Aspenall's Sweatbox."

Copied from one of the historical collections of pictures in the archives of Naval Lodge No. 87 in Vallejo, the Hall here shown is undoubtedly the Lodge Room that was occupied since its construction in 1866 on the site of the present Temple. Note the abundance of flags and wine. The East and South are clearly discernible.

CHAPTER XVIII

"MASONRY UNITES MEN OF EVERY COUNTRY, SECT AND OPINION"

CALIFORNIA LODGE NO. 1 and
LA PARFAITE UNION LODGE NO. 17

This beautiful Temple, at Van Ness & Oak Streets, San Francisco, is the home of California No. 1, Parfaits Union No. 17 and Occidental Lodge No. 22. It was for many years also the home of the Grand Lodge of California which is now at 1111 California Street. Occupied by California No. 1 since September 1914 this Temple is a credit to San Francisco, the home of many beautiful buildings, and to the Masonic Order.

Since those hectic days when twenty thousand fortune-seekers milled about in San Francisco in the year 1849, California Lodge No. 1 has been destined to take the lead to bring order out of chaos. Levi Stowell was a determined and strong leader whose gavel first banged down in the loft of a small building near the wharf on October 17 and started Freemasonry on a career not yet unfolded. In the maelstrom of funneling humanity from the hopper that was then Yerba Buena, barely out from Mexican rule, Levi Stowell and his fellow Masons set the tone that still reverberates to his eternal credit among the craft whithersoever dispersed across this burgeoning State.

It is fitting that a Charter dated November 9, 1848 in Washington, D.C. should be the one to originate around the Bay Area of San Francisco the gathering of Masons from every quarter of the globe, welding them into a cohesive unit that flowered into a Grand Lodge of Free and Accepted Masons of the State of California.

California Lodge No. 1 has ever been the watchdog of the craft in California. It was she who was instrumental in correcting otherwise deadly errors in establishing the proper regimes in the early days of our State history. It was she who, over the years, befriended the friendless and the homeless in the great melting pot by the Golden Gate. It is she who has furnished a great portion of the vitality and the personnel of Grand Lodge from its inception. She not only provided the first Grand Master, Brother John Nathan Drake Stevenson, but four additional ones since that time, and in addition has filled the offices of Grand Lodge from one end to the other with brethren of distinction and ability. And the reason is not hard to see. Her sons learn their Masonic lessons well, hence can impart them to others, greatly aiding the craft.

The purpose and determination to carry out the precepts of our art has been evident from that first meeting when eight members and thirty-six visitors headed by Colonel J. D. Stevenson of New York were crowded into that early room with the rafters supporting the roof so low that to address the East

The splendor of a bygone era, typified by the ornate doorway of this 1913 Temple built at the corner of Van Ness and Oak Streets in San Francisco, vies with the modern need for economic justification, as shown here on either side of the entrance to three wonderful early California Lodges, California No. 1, Occidental No. 22, and Parfait Union No. 17. Note the two California Bears and the beautiful bas-relief.

required three paces forward. Among the visitors were brethren from New York, Ohio, Maine, Maryland, Missouri, Tennessee, Alabama, Virginia, New Hampshire, South Carolina, North Carolina, Massachusetts, Florida, Illinois, Indiana, Kentucky, Louisiana and Pennsylvania as well as London, Nova Scotia and Canada.

The Centennials of California No. 1 are over. A child of the first centennial year would just now be about of voting age. The second hundred years has not only begun but is one fifth unrolled from the scrolls of time. And so we salute this Lodge of dedication and service as it moves into its second hundred years, "because Masonry must remain forever a progressive and moral science."

Ever since California's first master, Levi Stowell, gave fraternal treatment to one of the brethren of Le Progres de Oceanie Lodge of Hawaii by giving him a Masonic burial, and ever since California No. 1 raised another French brother, P. De Liagre, to the sublime degree of Master Mason, this premier Lodge of San Francisco has assisted and supported Loge La Parfaite Union No. 17 chartered on May 5, 1852.

And so a new and splendid Lodge began its labors, and to this day continues in its tradition in the French language to exemplify the great Lights which Masons revere.

It is a rare Mason in California who has not in one way or another heard of the "French Lodge," be it Parfait Union No. 17 in San Francisco or that "baby" Lodge begun as recently as 1897 in the southern portion of the State, Vallee de France, at Los Angeles. It is permitted by Grand Lodge to have its own ceremonial in the ritual of the Entered Apprentice degree, and it is of such striking beauty that Masons far and wide have traveled great distances to witness this degree. As Sherman in his history expresses himself, "the self-examination and stripping the soul as it were for preparation to receive the light of the truth of the Everliving God, in whom the candidate not in mere words alone puts his trust, but by ordeal before the Brethren proves in earnestness and reality that he has an abiding faith in God, a well-grounded hope in Immortality, full confidence in his brethren, and filled with love and charity toward all mankind but especially toward those of the Household of the Faithful."

The French Parfait Union means, of course, the perfect union, and such indeed has it been since its inception. The Masonic principles of liberty, equality and fraternity have never better been exemplified than in the annuals of this exceptional group of brethren.

However brief, we shall not omit one exploit of one of its illustrious members, gleaned from the pages of Most Worshipful Brother Leon Whitsell's account of this Lodge.

Worshipful Brother Alexander K. Coney, worshipful master of La Parfait Union in 1898 and 1899, during his youth was a member of the crew of a vessel docked in New Orleans and bound for Vera Cruz. One dark night he was accosted by a Dr. de la Boza who identified himself as a Mason in distress, wanted by the Mexican government. Brother Coney hid him aboard, but was chagrined to find boarding his vessel at Tampico, enroute, soldiers looking for Boza. Following exploits that ranged from a fist fight between himself and de la Boza to disguise his presence, to escape as a stevedore, Brother Coney later, upon arrival in Mexico City, was rushed to the Presidential Palace where he was offered a handsome reward for saving the life of the President of the Republic, General Porfirio Diaz. For Boza was he.

Only a loyal and true member of Loge La Parfaite Union could then truly say, "No, Senor, helping a Mason in distress is enough for me."

Decorators and architects have an affinity for old buildings; this important site of the birthplace of Freemasonry has been made a charming spot on old Montgomery Street in downtown San Francisco, being marked as an historic landmark by the State of California, as well as by California Lodge No. 1, Free & Accepted Masons at No. 726.

On this site on October 17, 1849, Levi Stowell first sounded a Masonic gavel in the upper story of a small waterfront building. In the one hundred and almost twenty years intervening, California in general and Freemasonry in particular have made great strides in accomplishment. A deft hand by an accomplished decorator has made this old spot today a joy to behold and a worthy showcase for marking the beginning of Freemasonry in the great Bear State. It is located at 726 Montgomery Street, San Francisco.

CHAPTER XIX

SAN FRANCISCO: HUB OF THE WESTERN WORLD

OCCIDENTAL LODGE NO. 22
GOLDEN GATE SPERANZA LODGE NO. 30 and
MOUNT MORIAH LODGE NO. 44

The City by the Golden Gate is a city unto itself and like no other. The Masonic Lodges spawned in its early days of growth and excessive vigor were, like it, composed of San Franciscans imbued with that verve and dash that its brisk sea air engenders. If you like it, no other spot on earth will do. If you do not, you're probably destined for Los Angeles.

Someone has said that San Francisco had no youth; it jumped from 600 to 60,000 in almost no time at all. So we will refrain from taxing your credulity by suggesting that you imagine San Francisco as a drowsy little Mexican settlement around the inevitable plaza, which of course it was, until the cry of gold went up, immediately followed by its population likewise.

Sam Brennan, one of the very early millionaires, not, however, in gold, but in real estate and merchandising, was one of those early pioneers of Occidental Lodge, having led the famous Vigilante Committee the year prior to 1852 when order began to emerge from chaos. Fire, which leveled the city, removed the last vestiges of the Mexican adobes. The continued arrival of three or more sailing vessels per diem added to the building boom, wharves, homes, businesses, churches, every appurtenance of a new city was on the march when Occidental Lodge No. 22 was petitioning for its charter. Unlike most Lodges no Dispensation was needed for this group of brethren, for a day or two later a Charter was issued, its birthday being May 22, 1852, the day the Grand

You will find no other photograph like this one of the home of the Most Worshipful Grand Lodge of Free and Accepted Masons of the State of California, showing the Pillar of the Porch and Columns leading to the Entrance. Who would have thought this multi-million dollar memorial to the labors of countless thousands of her sons would ensue from the union of four fledgling Lodges struggling amidst the wild melee of the early California miner's avarice and ambition?

When one compares the Building Directory, left, with the solid marble pillar standing on the Great Portico, the size and grandeur of this magnificent home of all Freemasons of the State of California begins to dawn upon him. Not ostentatious, yet rich in a degree fitting and proper, each Freemason of almost every Lodge in California, shouldered his proud burden of providing "one day's work" in its erection.

We do not anticipate that you will soon be requested to see him, but should you ever desire to see the Most Worshipful Grand Master of Masons of the State of California, and go to San Francisco to do so, this is the address and *this is the doorway to the Grand Foyer and the elevator which will take you there. It also leads to the Auditorium where Annual Sessions of the Grand Lodge are held.*

Master Hyam instituted the Lodge. One cannot help but wonder why this sudden deviation from custom. Actually, the list of petitioners was of much importance to the growth of San Francisco, containing a Past Grand Master from Kentucky, past masters of four Lodges, a Past Grand Secretary, plus eighteen stalwart brethren, as distinguished a group as could be found in all the west. This, plus the recommendation of all the Lodges of San Francisco, including that redoubtable one, California Number One, made it imperative for a Charter to be issued, which the Most Worshipful Grand Master Benjamin D. Hyam proceeded forthwith to do.

While the progress of Occidental Lodge has been the progress of the city and state in which it is located, many notables have graced its rolls. Far too many to recount, one by one. However, one of these must be mentioned, not alone for the uniqueness of his character but from the lovable and brotherly attitude expressed by those of his brethren who cared for him through his earthly span of years. And I am now referring to Joshua Abraham Norton, who was "Norton I, Emperor of the United States and Protector of Mexico" and who wore a colorful uniform, complete with sword and sash. It was his custom to issue checks on the "Imperial Treasury" for varying amounts for rent and the necessaries of life, and it was the custom of his brethren in Occidental to settle up for these checks wherever cashed. The "Emperor" proclaimed "decrees"—one of which was a command to the Central Pacific Railroad to build a bridge across San Francisco Bay— which "decree" was considered sane only after the elapse of many more decades. Over ten thousand persons passed by his bier upon his interment in the Old Masonic Cemetery at Turk and Masonic Avenue, in the year 1880.

Occidental, as did other early Lodges, occupied the beautiful Temple at Post and Montgomery Streets, a building approaching a Cathedral in its dignity and elegance, and one which took six or seven years to build, also one which was lost in the great fires of 1906 after the earthquake. In this building also we find Golden Gate Lodge No. 30, now Golden Gate Speranza.

Had it not been for H. G. Fredericksen, member of our third Lodge in this chapter, the charter and jewels of Golden Gate would have been irretrievably lost. And upon these jewels themselves hang an interesting tale.

It seems that Grand Lodge took umbrage, perhaps rightly, that this young Lodge should "squander" their substance by purchasing a twelve pound set of solid silver jewels, works of art, when they already owned an $18.00 set in good order and appearance. The brethren had each "chipped in" individually with silver to create this thousand dollar bit of display of opulence. Undoubtedly their pride in their Lodge prompted them. Seeds of dissension had been planted, however.

Forty-two members felt their financial interest was personal in those jewels, and it was decided to cast lots and the winner was to pay the loser one-half or five hundred dollars for the loser's interest. The Lodge won the determination by lot and paid its five hundred in order that the Lodge might now own the jewels in "fee simple" as our barrister friends would say.

The forty-two members then demitted and the Grand Lodge lifted the Charter for several months, picking up the paraphernalia which was returned to Grand Lodge. But the jewels sent to Grand Lodge were the $18.00 set and the Lodge, upon return of its Charter, has been able to this day to keep its beautiful ornaments. One of these jewels, and thirteen were made, not twelve, was a past master's jewel which the junior past master wore for one year, sitting on the right of the Worshipful Master in the East. It was first

GOLDEN GATE
MASONIC TEMPLE

This beautiful doorway will be found south of Golden Gate Park, and west of Twin Peaks, at 2404 - 14th Avenue, and is known as Taraval Hall, being on the corner of a street by that name. It is the home of Golden Gate Speranza Lodge No. 30, and Mount Moriah Lodge No. 44.

worn by "Uncle Billy," the first Master of Golden Gate, who was no ordinary Master.

William Schuyler Moses deserves a chapter, if not a book of his own. Born in Rochester, New York in 1827, he came to San Francisco during the height of the Vigilantes' activities. He was a wood worker and artisan of almost the genius class. He was a Mason whose entire life was entwined with his Lodge for all sixty-three years as a Master Mason, for in 1912 he still answered the roll call of past masters in Occidental No. 22, his date of return to the Supreme Grand Master being on December 9 of that year.

Two members that were raised in Golden Gate Speranza during "Uncle Billy's" three terms as Master were William O'Brien and James Flood, who became notorious as well as famous during the great silver mining days in Virginia City,

Nevada. Teamed with two other tycoons, these Irish brethren rose from a penniless condition when they arrived in the Golden State, to one of great affluence and wealth. Brother Flood and O'Brien opened a small restaurant where one listened intently while the other regaled the affluent patrons with Irish wit, soon they themselves joined the "manipulation of the market" and joined in the business of mining brokerage. Flood loved the ostentatious and built an elaborate home on Nob Hill not far from our present Grand Lodge home, circled it with a thirty thousand dollar bronze fence, kept shining by an employee engaged for this purpose alone.

Nor has this Golden Gate Lodge only been "unusual" during pioneer days. It again became noted for its "unusually fine" behavior when in 1966 Speranza Italiana or the "Hope of Italy" Lodge consolidated with Golden Gate to become

Home of two of the oldest and most honored groups of Masons in the western United States, Golden Gate Speranza No. 30 and Mt. Moriah No. 44. This building at the corner of Taraval and 14th Avenue was purchased by the brethren for a ridiculously low figure in 1940, and as a mortgage-free enterprise upholds the great American tradition of being "beholden to none."

Golden Gate Speranza Lodge No. 30.

Fore ninety-five year Speranza Lodge carried out the noblest aims of Freemasonry in the Italian language in San Francisco, being the third foreign language Lodge, La Parfaite Union No. 17 being the first, and Hermann Lodge being the second, in the German language. Speranza Italiana has been true to the principles and teachings of the fraternity and they continue to live on with their brethren of Golden Gate Speranza and have won a warm place in the hearts of all Brother Masons.

Along in 1853, just after Golden Gate had effectively received their Charter and put it to good use, another determined Mason arrived in San Francisco who led a group of others desirous of forming a new Masonic home in their adopted state. This leader was Philip W. Shepherd, and the group called themselves Mount Moriah in their Dispensation and were so designated in their Charter issued by Grand Master Howard on May 6th, 1854, being installed in due and ancient form by Benjamin D. Hyam, P.G.M., as Mt. Moriah Lodge No. 44.

The annals of Masonry will scarce record another gentleman as interesting in his Masonic career as its first Worshipful Master, Brother Shepherd. Born in England, his first initiation —he was initiated three separate times—took place in a cave near Alexandria, Egypt; his second in Kingston, Jamaica, because his work was so different from theirs, and his third initiation took place in New York. In each case his ship had

sailed before he could be passed. He petitioned California Lodge No. 1 upon his arrival in San Francisco for his Master Mason's degree after having been passed to the degree of Fellowcraft while stopping in Rio de Janeiro.

It is no wonder then that he imbibed freely at the fount of Mt. Moriah and became its first Master. Born in 1813, he died in 1865 after being elected Deputy Grand Master in 1958, 59 and 60. Interred in a San Francisco Cemetery of which Bro. Moses was Superintendent, some twenty years later his widow and Brother Moses disagreed as to his grave location, and when disinterred accidentally by a workman digging a drain, found a complete return to the dust of which each of us are composed. Except for two things, the bony skeleton and a silk handekerchief tied in a sailor knot. The silk was in perfect condition and after washing and ironing it caused the question to be put: "What is silk? Animal, vegetable or mineral?"

Many great and good men have passed the portals of Mt. Moriah Lodge in its more than a century of signal service to Masonry.

Nor has its age in any way crystallized into apathy. One of the finest of traditions of this fine Lodge on San Francisco Bay is that of the annual pilgrimage to other Lodges, far and wide, to share with them the peculiar advantages known only to Masons, in friendship, in fellowship, and in that charity of spirit which helps us grow better into fit inhabitants of that house, not made with hands, eternal in the heavens.

CHAPTER XX

"PIONEERS PREPARE THE WAY FOR OTHERS"

SAN JOSE LODGE NO. 10
and TEXAS LODGE NO. 46

In this building at 272 South First Street, San Jose, erected 1908, one of the oldest Masonic Lodges in the State of California, San Jose, No. 10, has held sway over the years. Now in the older section of the city, it has functioned as a beacon of Masonic Light, being organized July 11, 1850, two months before California became a State, and while its Capitol and Legislature were yet in San Jose.

It is with a certain trepidation that one launches a short paper to delineate the history of the "Mother of Lodges" inasmuch as there is a limit to which one can compress so much of an interesting and glorious past. In 1898, San Jose Lodge was seventh oldest of the Lodges in the State, and today she is still seventh, speaking well for our pioneer Lodges, all 100 of them chartered between 1850 and 1856.

San Jose Masons started out with a "bang" and they have been at it ever since. It is not unusual that in their earliest days they played such a determinant role in the early growth of California; their city was then the State Capitol, their members were members of its political bodies, their members were elected to delegate posts at the First State Convention, and their members were engaged in every good opportunity that came along in the growth and stability of Santa Clara County. It is not unusual that they were instrumental in founding the first center of learning, later to become San Jose State College, nor is it unusual that it attracted others of like mind to its ranks. It met twenty-seven times between the granting of is Dispensation and receipt of its Charter less than four months later on November 27, 1850.

Should we give at this point a list of real trail blazers, recognizing that all Lodges are composed of men, very few at this time would "ring any bells" with the average Mason who reads this account, except for members of San Jose Lodge No. 10, who, of course, will be familiar with their own background and heritage.

Yet there are several who should, for the imprint they left upon their day and time, and for the pleasure we derive with comparing their exploits to our own ideas of the temper of the times which prevailed in California's early days. One of these is William B. Almond, the Lodge's first Master.

Almond, scion of an old Virginia family, graduated with honors from a college back east. He studied law under a District Judge in Missouri. And he read Greek and Latin as we read daily headlines. But he loved the frontier, rising to rank of general in the militia. And he was a wag of the first water. He arrived in San Francisco just as the court docket was bursting at its seams, and Judge Geary appointed him head of a second court.

As Judge Almond, he chose to keep his knowledge and ability as a jurist to himself. But as a far western adjudicator of frontier justice he had no peer. He considered any lawyer a failure who did not present his lentghiest case, or argument for a client, in five minutes. He wore attire to suit the occasion: red shirt and galluses, jeans stuffed into his boots, unless he chose to remove one to pare a corn in open court with his foot on the mantel or nearby table. Some wit of the day wrote that Judge Almond could handle in twenty minutes any case a good lawyer could drag out six weeks.

No account of San Jose Lodge is complete without reference to Dr. Benjamin Cory. He was made a Mason in Ohio, receiving all three degrees in eight days. He helped organize San Jose Lodge No. 10, was its Master in 1853, and when he died had been a member over fifty years. This pioneer physician rode, of course, horses which he pushed over the plains in urgent strides to cover his Hippocratic domain that extended from Monterey on the one hand to Martinez, on San Francisco Bay, on the other.

And then there was William Henry Howard, our fifth Grand Master, who Chartered some fifty Lodges during his three terms, and then also there was William Alexander January, Master in 1868, printer, founder of newspapers, Grand Master of three York Rite Bodies, the Grand Chapter, Council and Commandery.

Each deserves a chapter; fleeting wings of time permit it not.

After working with the establishment of a new State in the throes of transition from an antiquated form of a patron government such as existed in California under Mexico to that of a modern republican form in which each citizen reckoned himself as good as the next man, perhaps a lot better, it comes somewhat of a surprise to find not more than forty miles to the south a Lodge with a name like Texas.

Yet in 1853 the forty miles could make a vast difference. Not so much in the level route followed by the flying hooves of the stages between San Jose, the State's Capitol, and the

This replica of California's first State Capitol Building is located in Santa Clara County's permanent fairgrounds and is a visitor mecca owing to its museum of artefacts appertaining to the transition from a truly Mexican center and village to the Garden City called San Jose. Many of those memorialized here, like Dr. Benjamin Cory, were pioneer members of San Jose Lodge No. 10.

cattle headquarters known as San Juan Bautista (for St. John the Baptist—in the adjacent County of San Benito), the little Holy Blessing, as Sherman puts it, but in the fact that we had not at that time achieved a universal cosmopolitan outlook on life in general. San Juan Valley was a world unto itself, an agricultural and a cattle world, while San Jose was urbane and staid by comparison.

Undoubtedly the Lodge was named for cattle barons from Texas. No one knows for sure. Certainly it was not named by the Flints who came to the valley soon after, for they were from down east in Maine. The father was a physician, but also ran cattle by the thousands. His son, Thomas, Jr., became our thirty-first Grand Master in 1897. Both father and son were Worshipful Masters of Texas Lodge No. 46 for fourteen years or more between them. The Flint family became so prominent in this Lodge that Sherman in his "Fifty Years" called it a flinty institution, and Whitsell in his "Hundred Years" repeated the pun. Of course the Flints were people to be reckoned with. Thomas, Jr. served California in the State Senate, being president pro tem, during three sessions.

Another pioneer of Texas Lodge, which incidentally was really more "Southern" than the name Texas might indicate, because it failed to elect until long after the "War between the States" a single member who was not southern born, was Mark Joseph Regan, and we are sorry he did not spell his name with another "a" in it. Regan became famous as a stage driver between San Juan Bautista and the connection point on the railroad, bringing sightseeing visitors to see the Franciscan Mission from every quarter of the compass. As a raconteur, he was said to have no equal.

He was made a Mason in Texas Lodge in 1872, but some time before this while riding his horse and taking a shortcut, he thought, via a long valley defile, was summarily stopped short by a man on a horse holding a Winchester .44 rifle who told him that route was closed. This angered him, but as he rode over the nearest crest he could see men in the defile standing in the form of a square. It was not until he was a member of Texas Lodge that he realized this was a meeting of his own Lodge, as its charter was one permitting it to meet as a roving Lodge within five miles of San Juan.

Texas Lodge No. 46 is a small Lodge, its membership will not even double its Lodge number, but it is proud, it is old, it has a glorious history behind it, and it views the world with that quiet equanimity it has earned through all its years of fidelity to its trust. It is now a part of a community marked as a point of interest and awe to a whole nation, because it displays to the world so carefully how a pastoral village could carry on a perfect blending of the best of two worlds, the old and the new.

Finis coronat opus—the end crowns the work.

This bronze plaque, placed by the Native Sons of the Golden West, stands under a tree opposite the site, now a parking lot near the City Library, where the building stood, pictured in bronze, that housed the Legislature of California during the years 1849-1851.
San Jose Lodge No. 10 was well represented, not only in the Assembly and Senate, but also in the First Constitutional Convention at Monterey.

This Southern type structure is the home of Texas Lodge No. 46 and housed at one time San Juan Bautista's Town Council. The Post Office has had its quarters here for many years, and on the left of the doorway is a good Village Museum. This was San Benito County's earliest Lodge, its Charter being dated May 6, 1854. In 1969 this building will be one hundred years old. Doesn't look it, does it?

Through this doorway have its members passed since 1869 to attend Texas Lodge No. 46, a pioneer Lodge that adopted the By-Laws of Davy Crockett Lodge (San Francisco No. 7) which gave it even more of a Southern atmosphere than the building itself seems to hint. Built at a cost of probably less than $5,000, Texas members assessed themselves according to ability to pay, and have owned it ever since. It is located in San Juan Bautista at Second and Mokulmne Streets.

The Masons of San Jose furnished many members of the early Legislature, men like William R. Bassham and Elisha O. Crosby to the Senate, and Dr. Benjamin Cory and Alexander P. Crittenden to the Assembly. This view shows a replica of the First State Capitol as it looked in 1850 when California assumed Statehood. San Jose remained the seat of government during 1849, 1850 and 1851.

CHAPTER XXI

"FRIEND, ADVISOR AND RULER OF INDIANS"

YOUNT LODGE NO. 12
and ST. HELENA LODGE NO. 93

Of the one hundred Lodges first Chartered by the Grand Lodge of California, only four have been given the name of individual brothers. Two of these are named for Presidents, Washintgon and Madison, and the third for a Grand Master, Howard.

George Conception Yount, born in North Carolina in 1794, reared in Missouri, and who lived much of his life in Napa Valley, was an exceptional brother and pioneer. In fact he created what amounted to a regal barony, comprising more than twenty square miles, ruling it with firearms and justice and with charity toward those whose lands he pre-empted—an Indian tribe called the Caymus.

He was a real pioneer, expert with the long rifle, at home with trapping sea otter, working at all the trades needed at Sonoma and San Rafael, where in 1836 he was baptized. Soon after he received a land grant which he called Rancho Caymus, to which was added another, La Jota. He found himself the only American settler between the Bay at Suisun and Oregon. The town which sprung up at his rancho came later to be called Yountville and it was here that Caymus Lodge No. 93 was Chartered in 1856.

First of course, we find George Yount being made a Mason in Benicia Lodge No. 5 in 1850. And one year later we find this benefactor of Napa Valley forming a Lodge at Napa, of which he held the office of Treasurer through 1854, after demitting from Benicia Lodge. He then joined Caymus Lodge and remained a member for the balance of his days. He may have joined the Catholic Church, but he also built a church for his area stipulating that it was "to be used by all denominations."

Yount Lodge No. 12 was still in the stage of being under a Dispensation when it recommended a Lodge to be formed at Sonoma, in the valley just to the west of Napa. This was done, the name being changed to Temple Lodge, taking the number 14.

It is interesting to find that George Yount was a close friend of General Mariano Vallejo, whose headquarters were in Sonoma. Since Yount came into the region soon after 1831 under the Spanish rule, Vallejo had ample opportunity to seek out his nearest neighbor. In so doing it is said that Vallejo found Yount and his men chipping shingles, that is they cut logs into suitable lengths, splitting them with the grain, to make shingles for the roof of the ranch house he was constructing. So taken with the idea was Vallejo that his new home and headquarters called Lachryma Montis, mountain tear, named for the Indian term "crying mountain" where a beautiful spring welled up, was shingled with the new style roof rather than the traditional Spanish tile idea.

No Lodge has had more ups and down than Yount Lodge No. 12. Yet it can boast no less than a Senior Grand Warden, a Grand Orator, and two Grand Masters. One of the last two, James B. Stevens, grew up in the Mother Lode, was made a Mason in Amador Lodge No. 65 in Jackson, was Master of Yount Lodge No. 12 for five consecutive terms, began as Grand Marshal of Grand Lodge in 1888 and became Grand Master in 1894. Both Brothers Knapp and McKinstry brought luster to Yount Lodge, perhaps more than luster, its existence could be attributed to their faithfulness, as it could to many another.

In 1865, Caymus Lodge moved to St. Helena and was granted permission to change its name to the same, retaining its number 93 on the register. No mention of this old Lodge would be complete without mention, in addition to George Yount who founded it, of Dunsdill B. Carver, who served it for so many years, being Senior Deacon four years, Treasurer for seven years, Senior Warden two years, and Master for eleven years. In addition to this service to his Lodge we just might add that he was one of God's noblemen.

It is certain that Freemasonry in Napa Valley will endure, being one of the bulwarks of freedom of our nation. The historical record of Yount and St. Helena Lodges is one of service, honor and blameless integrity.

Situated just opposite the historic Court House of Napa County, the home of Yount Lodge No. 12 is itself becoming a landmark in the County as a monument of its famous founder George C. Yount, pioneer and first citizen of the Napa Valley.

This early home of St. Helena Lodge No. 93, Chartered in the days of the Napa Valley Pioneer George C. Yount, when it left Yountville to come to St. Helena in 1865 it probably used this building, which is much older than it appears to be, with its new paint and altered window. On the sidewalk across the street is etched in concrete the fact that an adjacent building was the home of a G.A.R. Post. How many today know that GAR stands for the counterpart of the American Legion? (Grand Army of the Republic)

This home of Yount Lodge No. 12 was dedicated on August 29, 1889 and has served the Lodge well since that time, being still a sound modern appearing building and an asset to the community of Napa. It was not until 1887 that the use of real lambskin aprons came into use, in this Lodge, just two years prior to occupancy at this address of 1220 Second Street, Napa.

This copy from an old print of the Lodgeroom of St. Helena Lodge No. 93 is typical of the period known as the "gaslight era" as seen by the chandeliers to the right and left of the right hand pillar. This Lodge at St. Helena was begun at Yountville by George C. Yount who developed Napa Valley, and was until 1865 called "Caymus Lodge" after Rancho Caymus, a Mexican Land Grant.

St. Helena means grape country, and here is the home of St. Helena Lodge No. 93. Eight miles south is Yountville where the Lodge had its origin. This building now has passed out of the hands of Masons, note the left hand lower rental, but the "Richie Block" still boasts that there are Masons around. The older meeting place is just down the street.

CHAPTER XXII

"ALTA CALIFORNIA WAS A LOVELY PLACE"

TEMPLE LODGE NO. 14
and SANTA ROSA LODGE NO. 57

This is the fourth and last home of Temple Lodge No. 14, facing the Plaza in Sonoma. Its first home was the "Ray House" on the corner of Spain and Second Streets, its second home was destroyed by fire, and its third home lasted until the 1906 earthquake. The first meeting held in the above Temple was on April 19, 1910.

Few places in California have more nostalgic memories attached to them than San Diego, where California began, and Sonoma, where General Mariano Guadalupe Vallejo had his headquarters, on what then was "the Northern Frontier."

Yount Lodge in neighboring Napa, while still under Dispensation itself, signed the petition that brought Sonoma Lodge into being, Sonoma's original spelling being "Zanoma," and soon thereafter it asked to have its name changed to Temple Lodge. On May 6, 1851 its Charter was granted. At the time of granting, Sonoma was the home of the Pacific Division of the U.S. Army, with such notables stationed there as General Philip Kearney and Lt.-Colonel Joseph Hooker, of Civil War fame. We can only assume that the name change had something to do with the name "Sonoma" which in Spanish has a connotation with "sleeping" and the brethren of Temple Lodge decided it would never do.

While General Vallejo was a Mexican general and not a Mason, he was a colorful character and a distinguished gentleman who wished to see upper or "Alta" California taken over by the American Government. He had been sent to Sonoma to be a watchdog on the northern coast to observe what colonization plans were being undertaken by such countries as Russia, and to prevent them as much as he could. In 1846, a few years before the American settlers had achieved sufficient law and order to justify a Lodge's formation, the first Bear Party Revolt or episode took place. It was a rather spontaneous uprising of certain settlers among the Americans who would tolerate little oppression. They marched, all twenty-seven of them, into Sonoma one morning in June of that year, surrounded the house of General Vallejo, and took him and two other officers prisoners. Perhaps it is best to overlook the reception he gave them for purposes of discussion, which included some of the rarest if not also the most potent vintages this famous grape valley had to offer, and very nearly chalked

This historic building, used as an early Hotel, was built by General Vallejo in 1840 near the Sonoma plaza. It has housed many early notable guests as well as members of Temple Lodge, such as John C. Fremont, Kit Carson, pioneer Mason extraordinary, and the members of the Bear Flag Party. While early days were exciting, Sonoma was in general a law-abiding town. We doubt, without further proof, if the bandit Joaquin Murietta ever was a guest here.

up a victory for the old general. Several days later he was hustled off to Sacramento. The guard who remained, in securing the countryside, had a brush with Californios (Mexican forces) in which neither were especially gallant, but the Americans withdrew to Sonoma, where they fashioned the famous Bear Flag. They sensed they had no right to raise the stars and stripes, so invented a California Flag that we retain to this day, in essence the same as the State Flag. Among these men were of course Masons like Granville P. Swift who was elected sergeant, and Lieutenant George Derby who seemed to be in every bit of excitement anywhere in the state, and Dr. Robert Semple who had a part in the establishment of Martinez and Benicia Lodges.

The first Mexican native of California who became a Mason in this state was Brother Julio Carrillo. And his initiation into Temple Lodge again brings in Brother Derby who somehow managed to introduce a canard into our ritual by getting Carrillo to believe he was required to be branded along with all his livestock to identify himself as a true Mason. It was a prank others also entered with alacrity, burning cowhide with a hot branding iron under the nose of a blindfolded candidate while the application of a less hot iron upon bare flesh, gave vent to roaring laughter by our new brother when he saw what had really happened. It was a part of his Masonry he never forgot. Sometimes one wonders if a modern counterpart, if it could be employed, would not engender stouter hearts in this day of present enlightenment.

If you have followed the photographs accompanying the text you will know that fire and earthquake have taken their toll of Temple Lodge. It is an interesting fact that the Independent Order of Odd Fellows have a close affinity for Masons but nowhere more than in old Sonoma where they have traded Temples as fast as the other fellow's burned down. Each was

Losing Temples to outgrowth, fires, and in the case of Santa Rosa in 1906 which suffered more from the actual shocks themselves than San Francisco, from earthquakes, this new Temple, recently occupied, is the proud home of Santa Rosa No. 57, in which Luther Burbank was raised a Master Mason. It now houses a new Lodge named after him, Luther Burbank Lodge No. 752.

*Elbert Hubbard says that Andrew Carnegie only endowed two living Ameri-
cans by way of personal endowment, one was Booker T. Washington and
the other Luther Burbank, member of Santa Rosa Lodge No. 57 during the
latter years of his life. A new Lodge has been named for him and shares the
same Temple, Luther Burbank Lodge No. 752. Much of the fruit we purchase
in the supermarkets were improved by this wizard with plants.*

in the habit of permitting occupancy rent free because one
was never sure whose turn it would be next. Neither organization has been a large one but both have been tenacious
throughout the years. Temple Lodge started with eleven members at Charter time, going from about thirty in 1860 to forty
by 1890 and by 1930 had scaled the heights to a total of one
hundred thirty-three. Today, with the great upsurge of population and the increasing importance as a delightful tourist
center, Temple has a membership of in the neighborhood of
two hundred seventy-five.

The county seat of the county in which Sonoma is located,
the county of the same name, is the flourishing center of Santa
Rosa, the spot that Luther Burbank said was the "chosen spot
of all the earth as far as nature is concerned. The climate is
perfect . . . the air is sweet . . . the sunshine is pure and soft."

Sometime after George Horatio Derby, Lieutenant, U.S.
Army Engineers, had been the first master of Temple Lodge
at Sonoma, Santa Rosa was instituted under Dispensation by
Grand Master Howard in 1854. As many another, and like
Temple Lodge, Santa Rosa has occupied four Lodge buildings,
its second being rather a colorful structure of two stories,
the first floor being rented as the "Santa Rosa House," a hotel
noted far and wide for its hospitality. The hand-planed boards
and hand-forged nails were obtained from the East when, as
our local Santa Rosa Lodge historian says, they could have
been purchased for one-third less and would have been more
durable of local redwood.

Just after completing its new Temple at 4th and "D"
Streets, the earthquake of 1906 struck the city of Santa Rosa,
leveling its entire business district. Greatest examples of
brother to brother relief, as well as relief involving the Lodge,
have been demonstrated by this second Lodge in Sonoma
County. And not least among those beloved by every one who

knew him was the Tiler of Santa Rosa Lodge, Julio Carrillo,
once large land holder and rancher.

One other brother of Santa Rosa was born in faraway
Massachusetts and happened in his youth to read a work entitled "Variations of Plants and Animals under Domestication,"
which altered not only his life but yours and mine. I mean of
course, Luther Burbank, whose first job upon reaching Santa
Rosa was cleaning out chicken coops but who soon obtained
a small plot of ground. The remainder of this story we all
know. He was raised in Santa Rosa Lodge to the degree of
Master Mason in 1921 and remained during the remainder
of his life, until 1926, a devoted member.

In writing of these two historic Lodges located in the
beautiful valleys of the Sonoma and in one of the garden
spots of the world, we are not unmindful of the many brethren
who have devoted their days to their upbuilding, whose inspiration in their lives of great usefulness to their fellow man
was derived among the brethren of the mystic tie. If the future
holds the promise that the past has provided, there should be
no qualms as to our place in that distant day.

And so, we pause, without mentioning the names of many
brethren whose shining lives might be listed among the pages
of the glorious past, men like the Hon. Romualdo Pacheco,
State Treasurer, Lieutenant-Governor, Governor, Congressman,
Minister to Guatemala, and the second native Californian to
become a Master Mason. And brethren like Lindsley Carson,
brother of Christopher Carson, the famous "Kit" whose
knowledge and fortitude "saved the day" for the Americans,
was also a member of historic Santa Rosa. May the flowers
in the crown of Santa Rosa Lodge never fade, rather may
the luster the years add to them be reflected in our lives, and
in the lives of those worthy individuals who approach her
portals to share in this noble work.

CHAPTER XXIII

"I SHOULD LIKE TO KNOW WHAT YOU REALLY WANT!"

TEHAMA LODGE NO. 3,
WASHINGTON LODGE NO. 20,
SACRAMENTO LODGE NO. 40 and
UNION LODGE NO. 58

Here, at 12th and J Streets, Sacramento, are housed not only York Rite Bodies, but all the older Lodges of Sacramento concerned in these short historical sketches of the first 100 Lodges Chartered in the Grand Jurisdiction of California. The four so housed are Tehama No. 3, Washington No. 20, Sacramento No. 40, and Union No. 58, all of which were chartered before June 1, 1855.
While many pictures of Washington, as President, as a Mason presiding in the East, are to be found throughout this as well as other jurisdictions, it was here the author discovered a print of which there are but few, depicting General Washington standing at the Altar of Freemasonry with the sidelines fairly bristling with the great names of history.

It should not seem at all out of place that next in importance to Western Star No. 2 at Shasta, and to California Lodge No. 1 at Yerba Buena's mud flats, which later became the crisp city of San Francisco, there should arise the flourishing community of Sacramento led off by Tehama No. 3.

One does not utter the name of Sacramento in the scope of its beginnings without attaching the name of its founder John Agustus Sutter. When he was importuned to settle, at a modest price, for a perfectly stocked ranch in the Sonoma Valley to the north, he refused, and the owner, a Scotsman, angrily exclaimed, "Well, my stars, I should like to know what you really want!"

John Sutter *knew* what he wanted. He wanted a place where he would neither be required to doff his hat, as he put it, to a church, a flagstaff, or a military guard. And the eleven leagues in the Sacramento Valley, in spite of the fact it was in the domain of Colonel Mariano Vallejo, were *just* what he wanted.

He did not want, necessarily, the several hundred Indians, dressed appropriately in war-paint, he encountered on the banks of the river. Yet he charmed them into permitting him to settle.

Every reader of this short treatise will pick up the story from now on; the roaming herds of elk and deer in the grassy plain, the wolves in the farther woods; the settlement and building of "Suttter's Fort"; the coming of the eastern settlers down the branches of the American River which emptied near his settlement, and the subsequent cry of "gold" upon the banks at his mill-race in Coloma.

As the settlers poured in, members of the gentle craft poured in with them. Soon Lodges were formed in order that the needs for mutual support and charity to those unfortunate ones could be provided.

Few Lodges in our jurisdiction can compete with the heroic attempts made by early Sacramento Lodges. Many went under and surrendered Charters when they became hopelessly in debt. During the fall of 1849 and the spring of 1850, Tehama No. 3 raised from her only 69 members the unheard of sum of $32,000 which she expended in caring for the sick and distressed at a hospital she, along with the Odd Fellows, established at Sutter's Fort. Strong leadership of men like John A. Tutt, her first Master under her Charter, who became our second Grand Master, guided her affairs from choppy waters into calm seas. But some other Lodges were not so fortunate. She became the "Mother of Lodges" in the Sacramento Valley. Among those recommended for birth were Sutter Lodge No. 6 which soon expired in a welter of debt trying to succor the unfortunate ones pouring into the far west. Next was Washington Lodge No. 20 which turned out to be as astute as Sutter Lodge was unwise. Then she sired Sacramento Lodge No. 40 that has distinguished itself by a history nearly as satisfying as Tehama, its roster of "greats" being one of great honor.

In reading a short history of Lodges such as this one, readers should be made aware of the great gaps that necessarily are left behind in condensation. And of course, we intend no discourtesy to those Lodge historians of which every Lodge in our jurisdiction has at least one, by omitting the salient and vital accounting of their heritage. In particular, one feels this import in writing of the fertile Valley of the Sacramento where so much Masonic history was written, it being, as it was, the focal point of returning members from the mines who failed as well as those who succeeded.

There was however, one recent "find" made inadvertently in the foyer or anteroom of one of the meeting places of the Sacramento Lodges of which we speak. This was the picture, or lithograph, made from a chrome print in 1872 of General, also President, George Washington. Elsewhere in the margin the reader will find a reproduction of this print. It shows General Washington, gavel in hand at the altar of his Lodge in Alexandria, Virginia, with his tricorn hat in his left hand, with the open Bible before him, the square and compass laid thereon, the three lights arranged as they were in those times. On the east wall behind him is a portrait of General Lafayette, also a Mason in France, and on the right of the Master's Chair, another oil portrait of himself. Around the sidelines are shown in order, beginning from the south, first General Robert H. Lee of Virginia, next to him is Bishop White of the Episcopal Church, and next to the Bishop is the immortal Benjamin Franklin. Next to Franklin sits Robert Morris, who signed the Declaration of Independence and next John Mounts, and Roger Sherman. On the north side of the Lodge in the Treasurer's chair is Thomas Jefferson, third President of the United States, followed by Geo. Wythe and James Thompson. The appearance of Thomas Jefferson at once leads to the assumption that he was a Master Mason, not yet proven, but the publisher in 1872 at least thought it was he in his picture published at that time.

Washington Lodge No. 20 and Sacramento Lodge No. 40 have produced a number of great men, among them, James Anthony, the pioneer publisher of the Sacramento Union newspaper, and three governors of our State. First, Governor Milton S. Latham who also was a Representative and U.S. Senator. Next, Governor Romualdo Pacheco, third native Californian to join Masonry. And finally Governor Hiram W. Johnson, a native Sacromentan, who served five terms as U.S. Senator from California. Besides this these Lodges have produced that inimitable one-man Masonic institution, the redoubtable Nathaniel Green Curtis who served as Grand Master for the years, 1857, 1858, 1859 and 1860. He affiliated with Washington No. 20 after having been a lewis in Tennessee and Master of his Lodge before he was twenty-one years of age, perhaps the youngest Master of a Lodge in the history of the United States.

During the first five years of Masonry in California under

our Grand Lodge system, Union Lodge No. 58 was the sixth one organized in the City of Sacramento. It first met in a brick building belonging to another Master Mason by the name of Leland Stanford, at 56 K Street. The first cornerstone laid by the Grand Lodge of California was participated in by Union Lodge and its Master, James H. Ralston, delivered the oration. The cornerstone was put in place by William H. Howard, Grand Master, which became the County Court House at 7th and I Streets.

No account of Sacramento seems complete without noting that its location was unfortunate by way of flooding which occurred each spring when the American and Sacramento Rivers were at full flood. Stories are abundant telling how its location was selected, but it is a fact that the city perished more than once beneath the floods, Lodges being no exception. In December of 1861 and January of 1862 the levee around the city broke and travel to Lodge was by rowboat. Not only floods plagued the city but fire was common and in 1852 nearly wiped the city off the map. Another fire, in 1854, removed a large portion of the city along with the County Court House that was being used as the Capitol.

Yet in spite of fire, flood, and the machinations of the greedy and the profane public in general, the first railroad in California had been built, fast steamer service between Sacramento and the Bay Region was in operation, ferry boats at Carquinez shortened the time of travel, and progress demonstrated the skill and ability of Americans to conquer the problems facing them in their time. Members of the Lodges of Sacramento were a cross-section of every facet of life, from the water works, to the expanding levees, from the fire department to the building of homes and the establishment of new businesses; from stalwarts like George Tisdale Bromley, first conductor of the first railroad in California—Sacramento to Folsom—to William Cary Van Fleet, attorney, County Judge, Justice, California Supreme Court, and Judge of the U.S. District Court of Northern California. The Union Lodge, in particular, and all the others mentioned herein, carry on the tradition and standards that Masonry has set through the years to further years of usefulness and excellence in our Capitol City of Sacramento.

THE RED HOUSE, *famous in Masonic Annals of Sacramento, has almost become infamous because of its lurid associations, "owing to the unsavory character of the tenants on the lower floor, the Lodge soon moved to J Street between Front and Second . . ." In 1865 a new Temple was built at 6th and K and housed Masons of Sacramento until 1919 when the present temple was built.*

TEHAMA LODGE *No. 3 boasts rightly that she can show a closer descent from ancient Mother Lodge of England, than many another, for, on June 30, 1733, St. John's Grand Lodge, a Provincial Grand Lodge, under the Grand Lodge of England, was formed at Boston, than in turn on August 12, 1750 issued its first Charter to Hiram Lodge No. 1 in New Haven, Connecticut, which Lodge issued a Charter to Connecticut Lodge No. 75 "to several members about to journey to California in search of gold." This Lodge became Tehama No. 3 when Grand Lodge, which it helped to form, came into being April 12, A.L. 5850.*

Perhaps of only passing interest, this cornerstone marks the erection of the Masonic Temple at 12th and J Streets, in our State's Capitol, where for more than fifty years have gathered the great and the near-great of every class and office across California, to rest and refresh themselves at the fount of Masonry.

Every politician, of whatever stripe, plus thousands upon thousands of plain citizens of our State have crossed at this corner at the Senator Hotel in Sacramento where the State Capitol grounds reveal a glimpse of an office building and walkway leading to the Capitol itself.

The State Capitol of California at Sacramento
Built, designed, and inhabited by Freemasons since the
first Mason known to see California, Captain John Meek
in 1811 and 1812, has become the focal point of interest
for every visitor, Mason and non-Mason alike, to our
State's bustling city on the confluence of the Sacramento
and American Rivers.

CHAPTER XXIV

EVEN THE ALCALDE CALLED IT MARYSVILLE

CORINTHIAN LODGE NO. 9
ENTERPRISE LODGE NO. 70

This fine new plant, built within the past ten years, is the new home of Corinthian Lodge No. 9 at Marysville. None of her former locations are extant, Marysville being at the confluence of the Yuba and the Feather Rivers. Up until the time the great dams were built and the levees raised, floods were the cause of loss of many Marysville enterprises.

No city its size perhaps, at least none for which I can vouch in California, has had more annoyance, disruption and downright catastrophe than the city on the junction of the Yuba and Feather Rivers, named for Mary Covillaud, wife of the founder. This is the same Mary who was Mary Murphy of the Donner Party.

Because of the rampage of the rivers, levees have been raised higher and higher, and not until the great upstream dams, was the city of Marysville completely immune to inundation. Inspection will still show the hip-high curb stones in parts of town, and many houses had their first floors where most have second stories.

Enterprise Lodge No. 70 across the river has on occasion rescued the brethren of Marysville from their woes by supporting them with good hard cash after one of their recurring spells of being "wiped-out."

The stick-to-it-tiveness of Masons is nowhere better exemplified than here where no remains of former Temples or Halls exist where they have met from the day of their first inception in a tent at the corner, or near the corner, of Fourth and E Streets, as Lavely Lodge U.D. Jurisdiction of Illinois. This was before the formation of the Grand Lodge of California and probably was in February or March of 1849. Today, Lodges on both sides of the river have bounced back with new and imposing structures to house and further the cause of Freemasonry. History does not record why the Lodge at Marysville did not send delegates to the formation of Grand Lodge as others organized at the time did.

This new Temple, home of Marysville Lodge, Corinthian No. 9, had its cornerstone laid by the Grand Lodge of Free & Accepted Masons of the State of California on June 14, 1958. Modern in every respect, it furnishes the basis for the Masonic and social life of more than four hundred members of this pioneer Lodge of Northern California.

In fact, Marysville has had an interesting Masonic career for those who like to watch the peregrinations of brethren trying their level best in trying times to establish a permanent and suitable place to live for themselves and their posterity. Starting out as U.D. from Illinois, they first came under California law, Marysville No. 9. Soon another Lodge sprang up and Chartered as Yuba Lodge No. 39, and a little later a group of brethren calling their Lodge Independent Royal Arch Lodge U.D. became Chartered also as Corinthian Lodge No. 69. In 1874 consolidation took place and again in 1916 and today we have Corinthian No. 9, the brethren of the rootstock of all those around whom the toils of history swirled.

Through all of this, of course, certain names came to the fore. It is no one's intention to select a certain one detracting from the other. In some instances certain personalities were so strong, so resonant, so pervasive, that the Lodge itself could almost be said to be his reflection imbued with the spirit of the man himself. Dr. John R. Crandall was such a man in Marysville. He was also such a man in Lafayette Lodge which became later Nevada Lodge No. 13 of which he was its first Master. But then, he also was Master of Eureka Lodge No. 16 at Auburn, and at the same time was Senior Grand Warden of California.

And there are of course, others. Not only in Marysville, but in every pioneer Lodge of our Grand Jurisdiction they 26230—Galley 25 — —
come from the four corners of the United States. Stephen Johnson Field was such a man, whose name was carried on the first returns of Marysville Lodge, and who became one of the most distinguished jurists ever to grace the bench of the Supreme Court of the United States.

Any chronicle which can include a word or two concerning the entertaining story such as the "Life and Adventures of Joaquin Murietta, the Celebrated California Bandit," is sure to be appreciated. Hence it is worth mentioning that this book title by a man who usually wrote under the pseudonym of "Yellow Bird" published in 1854, was in reality none other than one John Rollin Ridge. Brother Ridge was passed to the degree of Fellowcraft in old Corinthian Lodge No. 69 and died as such in 1867 in Grass Valley.

Speaking of famous men of great character and strength, it will not be amiss to mention that one of the greatest was William C. Belcher, who was Grand Master in the Civil War years of '62, '63 and '64; was a member of Corinthian in 1859 but no one seems to be sure where he was raised. He became one of the most prominent lawyers in California, and served for twenty-eight years on the committee on Jurisprudence in Grand Lodge.

Across the river in Sutter County, Yuba City, more agricultural than mining in character, the brethren supported another Lodge that has, through the years, distinguished itself for being a "solid institution." While charity was responsible for ruining financially many Lodges which extended themselves unduly, both in Sacramento, in Marysville and elsewhere, Enterprise No. 76 was particularly careful to qualify each and every claim upon her generosity and therefore survived with a minimum of change or disruption from the even tenor of her way.

Here was a Lodge that minded its own business and was extremely careful about the quality of its membership. On one occasion a brother dropped a blackball for reasons best known to himself, then had qualms about it, stood up and announced the fact asking to change it. Since no one had left the room a new ballot was had. At the next meeting the Master called this ballot illegal and void. By dispensation of the Grand Master permission was granted to ballot again, and this time the candidate was elected.

In Enterprise Lodge on March 25, 1937, a father and four sons raised a fifth son. These were the Harter brothers. The father was Master in 1904 and present at the ceremony was the Master who, in 1900 had conferred the degree upon him, the father.

In a most businesslike manner filled with Masonic decorum, Enterprise Lodge of Yuba City has pursued the even tenor of her ways, and her ways have been those beyond reproach. Stabilized early in her career by one Caleb Wilcoxon, whose kindly spirit and eagle eye kept Enterprise on a very even keel, while he served her interests as Master for five years, as Secretary for five years, four years as Treasurer, and in 1874 as Tiler. All this while he was busy as Junior Grand Warden and representing his county as Assemblyman. Old Enterprise needs no further praise from this historian.

This old line drawing gives an idea of how the Feather River, the Yuba, and the Sacramento were important to Marysville. It was made probably after 1850 and 1857, and illustrated an old landmark called "Chiseler's Inn," originally called "Spring House." There was daily boat service between Marysville and Sacramento, about fifty miles.

ANTEDATING GRAND LODGE by several months, Masons of Marysville were active in March of 1849 by virtue of a dispensation to open a Lodge given John R. Crandall by the Grand Lodge of Illinois.

The accompanying notice does not state which Lodge, of which there were three, is having its cornerstone laid. There were Marysville No. 9, Corinthian No. 69 and Yuba No. 39. All these have consolidated into the present Corinthian No. 9, Yuba being the last to consolidate in 1916.

Trade center, depot for northern mines, named for his wife by Charles Covillaud who laid out the town in 1850, it first was called "Jubaville" by John A. Sutter, who, incidentally, was elected to take the degrees of Masonry in Marysville. No record exists that he did. His son, Emile V. Sutter, did, however, receive his first and second degrees here, and was raised in San Francisco.

The "Mission" type of architecture was prevalent in the first two decades of this century. This building, built in 1916, is the home of Enterprise Lodge No. 70 at Yuba City, Sutter County, just across the Feather River from Marysville, in Yuba County. Under strong leadership this pioneer Lodge looks to a bright future. Yes, that's correct: Marysville, County Seat of Yuba County; Yuba City, County Seat of Sutter County.

One of the prize possessions of Enterprise Lodge No. 70 at Yuba City is this original desk which has come through the years unscathed. Plainly visible are the volumes of Edwin A. Sherman, 33°, Editor of "Fifty Years of Freemasonry" published in 1898 by George Spaulding & Co., of San Francisco. Your author has relied on Sherman for many of his facts, and is indebted to him and to Most Worshipful Leon O. Whitsell, Grand Master in 1938, for much material forming this greatly condensed volume, drawn from his "One Hundred Years of Freemasonry in California" published by the Grand Lodge in 1950. No Mason should fail to read these four volumes.

This cornerstone, as the bronze plaque states, was located in Enterprise Lodge's first or second building at the corner of 2nd and Bridge Streets, Yuba City. Each could tell a story. Some of the story concerning the bronze may be apocryphal—even true stories have a habit of "growing" —but we are sure there must be Masons who recognize the first sentence as a true statement from the Holy Book.

CHAPTER XXV

IT IS AS EASY TO FIND GOLD AS TO PURLOIN IT

PLUMAS LODGE NO. 60

MOUNTAIN SHADE LODGE NO. 18

This is what one might call "a working Lodge" and while modest in appearance is the home of an earnest, loyal, devoted group of Masons in northeast California's Plumas County at Quincy. This is Quincy Lodge No. 60. Climatically on the cool side in winter, no deterrent has ever slowed the quiet constant loyalty of this group of Masons whose beginnings go back more than one hundred years to 1855.

When gold was discovered in Coloma, not every resident of California grabbed a pick and shovel. There were those grand old Californios, men of Spanish extraction, who had different ideas even when every storekeeper, merchant or whatever were leaving for the mines. Those who tilled the soil were the last to be influenced by the gold fever. One of those was said to have remarked, "My sons, God has given this gold to the Americans. Had He desired us to have it, it would have been ours before now. Plant and reap, let these be your gold fields, for all, while they live, must eat."

While Plumas County has yielded its share of the yellow metal, for even the famous John Bidwell had explored the upper reaches of the Feather River, perhaps the backbone of progress and permanency in the Plumas area can be said to be ranching and lumbering.

In any event an early pioneer whose name was Bradley acquired a large tract of land called the American Ranch. On it he owned the American Hotel, and since a few houses sprang up there he named it Quincy after his old Illinois home. He became one of three Commissioners for the County and first Master of Plumas Lodge and its leading spirit. Its first meeting after being Chartered on July 22, 1854 was held in his hotel but it was not long until the brethren decided to build, and their Lodge Hall was completed the following year.

This building still stands. It still is in use by the brethren of Quincy Lodge, and save for a slight extension of the Master's end of the building which once caught fire and was luckily extinguished, the building is much the same as when completed in 1855. It stands as the oldest building in the County Seat of Quincy, and one of the oldest Masolic Buildings of the State.

This team of oxen was the usual means of moving freight —other than by railroad—plowing a field or performing other heavy work. Taken in 1912 when logging required oxen, these citizens of Downieville, Sierra County, pose in front of the Mountain Shade Masonic Lodge. Bridge and porch have been replaced with newer ones shown in another photo. We are unsure that the present Secretary is here as a youngster, but he vouches for Homer Goald, Henry Schofield, Wm. McDougall, Perry Denmire, Thomas Griffith and Lawrence Shaughnessy. We hope that Norman Costa, good Secretary that he is, will forgive this indiscretion.

This is Mountain Shade Lodge No. 18 chartered May 5, 1852 and is the home Lodge of Leonidas E. Pratt, Grand Master in 1869, also in 1870, and in 1871 and 1872. Some of the original carpet, shown in Sherman's Fifty Years of Masonry's picture of the Lodge Room, still remains on the floor of the anteroom. With a membership around 60 Mountain Shade carries on a tradition of American tenacity for the better things of life.

The membership of Plumas Lodge has always had its fluctuations on long rising and long descending curves, reaching as low as only seventeen members in 1901, but thanks to John Daniel Goodwin and Arthur Walter Keddie and the coming of the Western Pacific Railroad, the swing was deflected again upward.

To this day Plumas is a small but very rewarding Lodge to visit. It is neither ostentatious nor pretentious. Its sincerity of feeling "comes through" to the visitor. But while small, it has boasted several names listed among the great of the California scene, and I wish to recount the story of one of these, a tinsmith by the name of Thomas B. Shannon.

Brother Shannon came to California during the gold days, and earned his keep as "Honest Tom, the Tinker" repairing miner's pots and pans. Sometime later he entered politics and became State Assemblyman, then he represented the Plumas and Butte District in the State Senate, the same year he found himself in Washington as a member of the U.S. House of Representatives. He even was a committeeman who accompanied the body of our martyred President Abraham Lincoln to Springfield, Illinois, on its last sad journey. He was a member of Plumas Lodge No. 60 from 1857 until he demitted to San Francisco, upon his return from Washington, from which place he again was elected to the California Assembly.

While events were taking their course in the upper reaches of the Feather, over the mountains not more than thirty air miles to the south, but in an entirely different world, nestled in the fastness of the upper Yuba River, lies the smaller town of Downieville. It too is a County Seat, yet what it lacks in quantity it makes up for in spirit and the independence of mountain men everywhere.

Named for one William Downie, it was one of the many locations of a gold strike that attracted thousands to the site.

By the spring of 1850, Tin Cup Bar was so named because one was filled each day by a miner with gold! A year later the population was five thousand, and it had a Masonic Lodge.

Today it has fewer than five hundred probably and one can easily read between the lines to reconstruct the history of Mountain Shade Lodge. Its name does not readily lend itself to records yielding its origin, but it is easy to assume that from its location in a town nestled among towering mountains and shade cast by the mountains came early to the folks of Downieville.

Fire and flood have been the lot of Downieville. Yet through every change of fortune the Lodge at Downieville carries on, having fluctuated in numerical strength from its present some sixty members back through the lean years to as low as less than thirty. Fifty Master Masons were on its roll in the year of its Charter in 1852.

The size of any Lodge is not necessarily indicative of the quality of its members and few Lodges give greater assurance than this mountain retreat, for from here came one of our early Grand Masters, Leonidas E. Pratt, the second to serve four consecutive terms.

After a "go" at mining, Brother Pratt assumed his profession of the law of the 17th Judicial District and two terms in the State Senate. He was Master of Mountain Shade Lodge in 1865, 1866 and 1867 being Grand Orator of Grand Lodge in 1865.

Mountain Shade also produced another dignitary, the Grand Master of the State of Nevada, George W. Hopkins, who served as Secretary of Mountain Shade in 1852, and who moved from Lodge to Lodge as the vagaries of the search for gold may have dictated.

The snow comes early to the mountains, so we must hurry on, before the reader beds himself down until spring.

CHAPTER XXVI

A MIGHTY METROPOLIS WAS OUR FORTE

LOS ANGELES 42 and HAWAIIAN NO. 21

Inasmuch as Los Angeles and San Diego communities were both originally Spanish and Mexican in character, and inasmuch as the mixture of Americans with adventurers from all parts of the world were added to the mixture upon the discovery of gold, it is no wonder that both these cities were considered dangerous places to live unless you were able-bodied and could take care of yourself. In fact, Los Angeles, in the early part of the 1850s was considered the toughest place in the world.

Lurid stories are not, as the reader has found out by now, the main feature of the accounts of exploits of this condensed history of the early Lodges. Yet Los Angeles, because of the character of its growth, contains several accounts that must not be overlooked simply because of their western flavor. One must not give the complete impression that the members of these early groups of Masons were of such sterling character that none were ever caught off-base.

Therefore, and with no apology for facts as they have been handed down to us, we find that "Old 42" was organized by a meeting in the office of Myron Norton, a member of the bar, on March 16, 1853, followed by the granting of a dispensation in October and the following May of 1854 the Charter was issued. The first Master was Hilliard P. Dorsey, a southern gentleman among southern gentlemen who formerly served in a Mississippi Regiment under Jefferson Davis. This accounts for his plan of living and his great care to keep his name and honor unsullied, as was customary in the time he lived. However, the free and breezy way of the far west was to be his Masonic undoing. Standing in a doctor's office he was fired upon by one Racey Bivins of San Joaquin Lodge No. 19. The bullet missed and the upshot resulted in a duel in which both were wounded, and after being warned not to duel by the then Grand Master, both Dorsey and Bivins were expelled from the fraternity. His fiery temper led to a quarrel with his father-in-law, also a member of Los Angeles No. 42, who later shot him dead.

Just to take this sour tastes out of our minds let us turn to another southerner, Thomas Foster, who was as much a credit to the Lodge as its first Master was a disgrace. Foster was a physician and the Lodge's first Junior Warden. He was married to a fine Scottish lady and their home was headquarters for people of consequence in the little community of Los Angeles. Strange as that sounds, Los Angeles, the city, in 1853 was scarce more than a few houses around the old plaza, had a population of something over fifteen hundred, and if you counted the whole county, including Orange County, you may have reached thirty-five hundred, but this included some three hundred "domesticated" Indians, a few negroes, two Chinese and one Hawaiian. The only industry was saddle making, vineyards in long rows led in every direction, and ten miles eastward, on the bank of the San Gabriel River, was the next settlement.

And then there was an early member of the Lodge, W. G. Dryden, whose decision as local Judge has come down to us with a certain flourish. It seems that the County Sheriff had married the daughter of an influential native, and in his official duty brought to justice the leaders of a local band of horse thieves and bandits. The leader turned out to be his wife's brother. At the trial Judge Dryden pronounced, "The jury finds you guilty as charged," but after a long lecture, recommended clemency and announced, "therefore I declare you a free man, you may go about your business." Someone in the courtroom asked, "What *is* his business?" Never flinching, the Judge replied, "Horse stealing, sir, horse stealing!"

To keep the record straight, most of the recounting of events retold in this chapter are taken from the account developed by Most Worshipful Whitsell in his "One Hundred Years of Freemasonry in California" and are condensed so far as practical for this short accounting of the early days. We heartily recommend the reader to the full history. Speaking of early days keeps in mind that in Los Angeles at this time its population lived in an arid semi-desert, a barren waste, and even though fertile, was completely without water. Trees were absent, even the hardy California pepper tree was not set out for the first seventy years at least of American colonization. Only cactus, greasewood, and the flora indigenous to the stories of Zane Grey were in great abundance. Any river in season was of course full and some unfordable for days. Travel was what we would call "an experience."

Were we to give an accounting all the great and good men who have graced the halls of Masonry in Los Angeles, in this, "old 42" or in all her many Lodges, there would grow a great list of names and a solid volume of accounting their exploits. We can rest assured that the members of this and subsequent Lodges had a great deal to do with the early development of the City of Los Angeles as well as its phenomenal growth. Public schools obtained a firm foothold by their kind offices. In the two cities mentioned, the Masonic Lodge was the very next institution to come to life after the establishment of the American government. Churches and schools came later. The Lodge, as we can well imagine, greatly stabilized a very wild and dangerous country. Masonry itself was planted amongst the earliest of pioneers. Men like Isaac Williams and Ben D. Wilson and J. T. (Juan José) Warner of Warner's Ranch fame, who had some claim to Los Angeles No. 42 and later our Governor during the Civil War days, John G. Downey, who did so much to make the cornerstone laying of our State Capitol an outstanding occasion, was a distinguished member.

The first of the pioneers were really the seafaring ones who most early sailed the coast of California, and one John Meek, who was believed to have done so as early as 1811 but who in 1843 was a charter member of the first Lodge to grace the Sandwich Islands, Le Progres No. 124 under French rule, and also was an organizer and charter member of Hawaiian Lodge No. 21 under the jurisdiction of California. Men like John Meek and John Paty and William Heath Davis, Jr. made a Lodge in the Islands, now our forty-ninth state, possible.

It shall be impossible within the limited space at our disposal to recount to you the full story of Freemasonry in the Hawaiian Islands.

If we can but assess enough since that day in 1842 when Captain and Monsieur M. Le Tellier was enabled to establish his Le Progres de l'Oceanie followed by our own Hawaiian No. 21 of which Samuel Lyon just ten years later became first Master, and give you sufficient impetus to explore its captivating and moving history, it will suffice. For the royalty of the Islands themselves became Masons, and this alone lends an air of mystery, of charm, and of lasting value to the responsibility of the growth of the people of this Island Kingdom, that will captivate the reader. For the best account, either that found in "One Hundred Years" or "The Establishment of Masonry in the Hawaiian Islands" compiled by C. F. Chaussee, P.M. are excellent.

To further the reader's interest, be reminded that the even tenor of events in Honolulu were always flavored by many circumstances, that while legitimate and not unexpected among those who come from the four corners of the earth, the interplay of events in the growth of a population mixed with the native, the Asiatic, the European, and to us the exotic far East and the Levant, produce a Masonic potpourri not to be underestimated by those who enjoy the interplay of history.

This is a close-up of the old doorway of Los Angeles Lodge No. 42 at 416½ North Main Street. The restored facade of the original Pico House adjoins the next building, the Mercedes Theatre with the iron doors, used by settlers as a fire break as well as security.

On the right of the First Theatre in Los Angeles is Los Angeles Lodge No. 42, the second Masonic Organization to be established south of Tehachapi Mountains on May 5, 1854. This is No. 416½ North Main Street. The Old Plaza is one block south (to reader's left).

The Pico House, in process of restoration, in the old Los Angeles Plaza. On the far right can be seen the edifice housing Los Angeles Lodge No. 42 on Main Street.

Sorry about that last sentence being so long. Study it, and perchance it will pique your interest to enjoy the curling waves, the smooth sands, the gently waving palms beneath the star-decked heavens of Oahu where your brethren of the mytic tie are to this day carrying on the traditions of yesterday. No needy brother has ever gone empty handed from the doors of Hawaiian Lodge No. 21.

CAPTAIN JOHN MEEK

One of the founders and a charter member of Hawaiian Lodge. Born at Marblehead, Mass., November 24, 1791, he arrived in Honolulu in 1809, and returned in 1812 to make his home. He became a farmer interested in blooded stock. As master of the Don Quixote about 1832 he imported a bull and three heifers from San Francisco, which formed the nucleus of the vast herds of cattle in the islands today. He died in Honolulu January 29, 1875, and is buried here. His descendants still live in Honolulu.

This is the Lodge Room of Hawaiian Lodge No. 21 as it appeared just before the turn of the Century.

This modern plant of Hawaiian Lodge No. 21 in Honolulu carries the Egyptian motif and possesses a flavor that is typically American yet has not quite lost its oriental touch. The brethren of our sister State are proud of their wonderful heritage.

CHAPTER XXVII

"GEMS OF THE NORTHERN MINES"

MADISON NO. 23, GRASS VALLEY

ILLINOISTOWN NO. 51, COLFAX

NEVADA CITY NO. 13

GRAVEL RANGE NO. 59, CAMPTONVILLE

Taken from the steps of the U.S. Post Office in Grass Valley, this Masonic Temple housing Madison Lodge No. 23 typifies the organization's long ability to progress and flourish. It has lately begun a program of study which will lead to restoration of much of its history from old prints, photos and mementos, the originals belonging to the Lodge having been lost in many ways, the ravages of time, and fire.

Not that there were not other "gems." Perhaps Grass Valley is the most qualified to hold the honor, just as Columbia City in the more southern part of the lode holds that honor. Both were hard rock centers, where men could work underground in the quartz veins. Both established Lodges that flourished, Madison No. 23 being at the present time a most active and important group of Masons, as she has been through the years. Chartered in 1853, she sustained the complete fire that wiped her out two years later. However, her growth and prosperity has sustained her. In 1928 again she was ravaged by fire, and she lost everything. That Madison today is a vital and strong organization is a tribute to her members.

The best descriptive fragment that has come down to us concerning the early days may be quoted verbatim from Brother Sherman: "Madison Lodge being located in the heart of the gold quartz mining region of Nevada County, the greater portion of its members have been and are still engaged with sledge and drill . . . go down into the deep shafts and along the chambers and you will meet Brethren . . . stripped to the buff, perspiration issuing from every pore . . . then go to the Lodge room at night, and there, dressed in the garb of gentlemen of elegant leisure, you will find these same Brethren in the East, South and West and around the hall, conducting the affairs and ceremonies of Masonry with true politeness, dignity and skill, as if they were professors . . . these brethren can handle the gavel and trowel with the same skill and facility that they do the sledge and drill."

This plain facade houses the warm hearts of those members of Gravel Range Lodge No. 59 at Camptonville who took in the members by consolidation of Forest Lodge No. 66 in September of 1955. Both Lodges are early day mining Lodges, Forest No. 66 being nearly one hundred years at Allegheny City, east of Camptonville. Fire and attrition have been the great levellers of these mountain Lodges, brave to the last man. This new Temple signifies their determination to make the future outshine the past.

This building directory, or trestleboard, with the keystone in its curved top, is an old one. So also is the wrought iron ornamental light box above it, both restored by the members of Nevada 13, indicating that this group of dedicated Masons are alert to change and growth. Its Lodge Room possesses a warmth that few achieve and well reflects the principle of the ashlars.

Illinoistown had the first Lodge hall which was reached by a staircase consisting of three, five and seven steps. And that is not all that is unusual about this mother lode Lodge. First, of course, it was located at a very rich site and the argonauts from the mid-west were the most prevalent, hence the name Illinoistown for town and Lodge which moved a short distance across the railroad to Colfax, a stone's throw. Maybe being a railroad town has an effect on people who live there, in any event No. 51 has been aptly called a Lodge consisting of "individuals" and its history is is replete with the unusual. The story most often told is the year elections were held a month previous to the proper time, electing a full slate of officers, then, having second thoughts, holding another election at the proper time and defeating all the victorious candidates of the previous election.

Yet we must not think Illinoistown Lodge was profligate or rough in character. Its history does not bear this out. For example, when a brother entered apprentice had moved to Ventura and the Lodge at Ventura asked permission to complete his second and third degrees, Illinoistown was hesitant about granting same until they assured themselves that he was treating his wife in a better way than he did when living in Colfax.

All of the Lodges of which we are speaking are located within a small circle whose diameter is not more than twenty or twenty-five miles, even though Colfax is on the main freeway route between Sacramento and Reno, and Camptonville is off the main traveled thoroughfare between Grass Valley and Downieville on the famous 49 Route of the Mother Lode.

Just north of Grass Valley is the well preserved small city of Nevada, although the new freeway has just cut Nevada City into two parts, and for some impaired its former charm. Yet much remains and included in her past is the splendid story of Nevada Lodge No. 13. Beginning as Lafayette Lodge under a foreign jurisdiction (foreign being a Masonic term meaning other than California), it had scarcely functioned until fire wiped it out completely in 1851. But the next year it conferred more degrees than any other Lodge in the Jurisdiction, a total of one hundred, consisting of 37 entered apprentices, 33 fellowcrafts and 30 raised to the Sublime Degree of Master Mason. Nevada Lodge has been a bulwark

After three disastrous fires, this hall, built in 1864, has served through the years as the home of Nevada Lodge No. 13 at Nevada City. The entrance is at the extreme right in the photo partly hidden by the power pole. The best balanced, preserved, and displayed library and collection of early artifacts one will encounter in the mother lode will be found in this early building, at 108½ Pine Street.

Mrs. W. G. Groves, where Lester Pelton boarded, sewed for miners on very heavy material, and for this reason Pelton designed the first improved water wheel and installed his first for her about two feet in diameter on her sewing machine. The monument, above, stands on the spot where the wheel was invented, and was dedicated by Grand Lodge for the brethren of Gravel Range, Camptonville, who provided it in Brother Pelton's memory.

of good in Nevada County. She has produced no less than two Grand Masters, one Senior Grand Warden, two United States Senators, two Justices of the California Supreme Court, the first County Judge of Nevada County as well as an array of other men of high office and probity—when probity was a word relating to politicians.

The office of County Judge can scarely be mentioned without a few words concerning the first one, Thomas H. Caswell, who stood off a lynch mob and tricked them into assisting the law to give a proper trial to one Brown who had shot and killed a man named Smith in true western fashion. When our hero, the Judge, stepped from the hotel to plead for Brown's proper trial the cry of "Hang the Judge" was nearly heeded. Following this, he became a most favored and honored man, later became Master of Nevada Lodge and Grand Lecturer of Grand Lodge. From this he became Grand High Priest, Grand Commander of the Grand Commandery, and in 1895 held the post of Grand Commander of the Mother Supreme Council of the World of the Ancient and Accepted Scottish Rite to achieve the greatest number of honors ever awarded a Mason of this State. No man, says Whitsell, could have held them more graciously.

Camptonville lies on the outer edge of the diameter of the circle containing these four mother lode Lodges. Today it is a sleepy village, the home of Gravel Range Lodge No. 59, the new Lodge of William Bull Meek, who achieved notoriety in his own time and fame in ours, and but for whom and the life of Lester Allen Pelton, inventor of the Pelton Water Wheel, the history of Gravel Range No. 59 would undoubtedly have been changed.

Those of my readers who are familiar with the term "E Clampus Vitus" will have no trouble recognizing William Bull Meek for the type of man he was. Those who are mystified by the term, suffice it to say that however rough and ready its disciples may appear, its purposes have always been laudable and the good done by this group of "highbinders" is out of all proportion to the pranks, the coarse and ready wit cherished by its members. No better example of the heart of gold in the rough exterior of a mountain man, miner, mule skinner, merchant and member illustrious of Gravel Range Lodge can be found than Bull Meek.

This largest of the Water Wheels, being 30 feet in diameter, was used to compress air for use in the North Star Mine at Grass Valley. Most efficient wheel of its type ever developed it was invented by Lester Allen Pelton who joined Gravel Range Lodge No. 59 in 1869. The mine which this wheel served reached a vertical depth of 4,000 feet, the deepest at Grass Valley.

This "Clampatriarch" William Bull Meek, longtime member of Gravel Range Lodge No. 59 at Camptonville, has here been honored with a large granite monument upon which the above bronze plaque bears out his colorful history as "stage driver, Wells Fargo Agent, Mule Skinner, Teamster, Merchant." Men like Brother Meek have kept Masonry alive in many a remote area. After the bloom had faded from the gold dust the trowel continued to spread the cement known to Masons.

The high schoolers of Colfax, Nevada County, enjoy having their records made in this photo of the old building housing the Lodge on the main street opposite the railroad station. Illinoistown Lodge No. 51 has weathered the years of changing times brought by the declining mines, the building of the railroad, and of late the lumbering and grazing industries and the influx of urban families seeking the "quiet life."

CHAPTER XXVIII

A TRIBUTE TO FIDELITY AND PERSEVERANCE

FORBESTOWN LODGE NO. 50
ROSE'S BAR LODGE NO. 89

Meet Burt Mansell, P.M. Master in 1931, holding the deacon's rods with their curious designs, left, and Charles Van Zant, Secretary, both of Forbestown Lodge No. 50, right, holding the Steward's rods with the corn and wine designs, and wearing the old jewels of office. Burt is 87 years young, very active, and he and Brother Van Zant somehow remind us of other stalwarts of this fine old Lodge. The jewel collars are handcrafted of solid silver and are works of art.

Forbestown today is a lumbering area and a forgotten bit of history. Could we but make it come alive, what a story it could tell of the pioneers from Maine to Missouri, of the miners and the highway robbers, and of gold and of Wells Fargo and the Concord Stages to Marysville and Oroville. Located twenty-five miles east of Oroville in Butte County on the south fork of the Feather, it is without doubt one of the more colorful and nostalgic of locations for a pioneering Lodge of Masons whose fidelity and perseverance know no bounds. And today it is stronger than ever, not only because of its glorious past and the curiosity and interest from afar, but because the whole territory of Olla Batt, who in 1935 owned the whole town location, and of Bidwell's Bar, and of the entire area from Grass Valley to Quincy, is coming to life as California grows in population, and interest accelerates.

Smartsville and Forbestown are but twenty miles apart in direct line. Smartsville lies just off the road running between Marysville and Grass Valley, and is just a piece up the old road from Timbuctoo. It is near Park's Bar Bridge and Rose's Bar on the north fork of the Yuba River. Forbestown is on the south fork of the Feather in Butte County. Both were Lodges resulting from the development of the gold fields, and owing to hydrolicking both eventually played out and people moved into other areas. Great pressure has come to bear on both these old Lodges to consolidate and move elsewhere, but both have successfully resisted the easy solution to their difficulties, and both have won through to a bright future in the annuals of Masonry in California.

Those who cull honors and curry favor will like Rose's Bar the least for these brethren throughout the years from the day of receiving their Charter on May 8, 1856 have done but one thing successfully: kept the fires of Masonry burning and minded their own business. Through good times and bad the brethren of Rose's Bar have held tenaciously to their business

115

Justly jealous of their prerogatives, the members of this Temple are solid citizens who live and work away from urban centers, away from the teeming crowds, but who have made for themselves here a social and fraternal home worthy of the strenuous lives they lead in a modern age. With electricity and butane gas, this Temple boasts every modern convenience along with a Lodge Room mellowed by more than one hundred years of fraternal intercourse of give and take, lean and good years alike. Such is the home of the brethren of Rose's Bar No. 89 in Smartsville.

Here is a building that belies its age. Its newer vintage is enhanced by the new porch built by the brethren of Rose's Bar Lodge No. 89 in 1953. The building you see here was constructed before 1858 because in that year it was purchased for $500 and has ever since been in use by these Masons of Smartsville who have resisted all change or loss of Charter. Beginning with a membership of 27 they now boast nearly 80.

of living the life of moral rectitude to the best of their ability without fear or favor, ignoring the world of fuss and feathers, action and progress, but when occasion required not being above adding a name or two to the lists of their deceased brethren that would permit them in reduced numbers to carry on as a Lodge.

Their Hall to this day is intact. It was purchased for $500 in May of 1858, after disposing of the old one for $75.00, and today in 1968 it shows only the care and use of a normal habitation that is loved and cared for. In entering its Lodge Room one leaves the world of the century and enters a long-forgotten era, yet, below stairs, a modern plant is in evidence for refreshment and entertainment. And Asa Fippin, erstwhile Secretary of the Centennial Committee, who opens its doors with pride, is living proof that the principles of Masonry are not only for the hurrying people of the teeming metropolis afar, but also for those whose hands have toiled in the forest, the mine, and the field.

Forbestown, on the other hand, one is informed, was a camp of fifteen hundred population, and "more dissolute than any in the state" and competed with places of low reputation such as Murderers' Bar, Whiskey Slide, Hell-out-for-Noon, and many another. Here on May 3, 1854 Forbestown Lodge No. 50 was chartered. Here in 1865 we find in its minutes that "whereas on the evening of 14th April, Abraham Lincoln was murdered by a dastardly assassin at the Capital of the Nation, and whereas the dictates of patriotism and respect

we bear towards the honored dead, be it resolved that the Lodge be clothed with the emblems of mourning, that these minutes be spread upon the records of this Lodge, and the Secretary furnish the Oroville and Marysville papers with a copy of these resolutions for publication." Which is ample proof that evil doers get publicity, but the good is often interred with their bones.

The story of Forbestown Lodge is one of a long battle against extinction.

To make the story graphic and jump into the middle of things, let us begin this story by recounting the antics of one Charles Francis Adams and one William John Schultz, the latter of whom was Master of Forbestown Lodge for twenty-nine consecutive years beginning in 1896 and extending unbroken until 1925. In many of these years these boys would strap their packs on their backs and tramp over the mountains ten miles to Lodge. Being the only ones there, at seven-thirty, Brother Schultz would assume the East, and Brother Adams the West, then in a running play they would open Lodge, Adams answering from each station as he ran around the room to fill all the offices. Then they would transact what business had to be done, close Lodge the same way and sleep in their sleeping bags by the old pot-bellied stove, trudging home again on the morrow.

As the various Lodges of the mining areas of our State began to fade because of the leaving of derelict towns in the

In this building Worshipful Masters like Gaylord Smith Wilsey Twogood, and Andrew Jackson Hankins, and Ralph Waldo Emerson, and Thomas H. Dodson taught the lessons of Masonry, not to mention men like William J. Schultz who was Master for twenty-nine years, and Charles Francis Adams, and Jeremiah Ames Vaughn by whose labors through many lean years the old Lodge maintained its good standing in the California Jurisdiction.

Burt Mansell and Chas. Van Zant open Forbestown Lodge No. 50 for visitors' inspection. Burt has been a Mason most of his life and is now eighty-seven years young. He was Master in 1931. Charles has been a Mason now about three years and is Secretary of the Lodge. A warm welcome awaits any visitor, and contains many surprises, by way of Lodge activities, furnishings, pictures, utilities and appointments.

In the front wall of Forbestown Lodge No. 50 this marble marker has finally found a permanent resting place after serving brethren of both fraternities in the mining town of St. Louis, Sierra County. It was related by Jesus Bristillos, whose son Joe is a Past Master of Jefferson Lodge No. 97, that this slab was brought in by pack mule in the early 1850's.

mountain coves, Forbestown over the years absorbed by consolidation no less than four other organizations of Masonry: Polar Star Lodge No. 90 at the Forks of Poor Man's Creek; St. Louis Lodge No. 86 at St. Louis, Sierra County, the one in which Downieville is the County Seat; Gibsonville Lodge No. 158, same county, and Jefferson Lodge No. 97 at Rabbit Creek. The latter location was fastened to history not only by the richness of gold pockets but by being where little Lotta Crabtree learned the songs and dance-steps that made her famous from Mariposa to Weaverville.

One of these Lodges joining Forbestown Lodge, St. Louis—produced an artifact worthy of note that adorns the face of the building as a marble tablet, weighing over 300 pounds and freighted into the mountains by muleback after crossing the continent from Vermont or even Italy—no one is sure—and which, after being abandoned and hydraulicked down the sluices, was recovered for a doorstep, finally re-discovered and placed in its present position of honor. No less important are the officer's jewels, and as unusual, being made of silver from Virginia City, Nevada, by the Treasurer of Gibsonville Lodge and acquired by Forbestown at time of their consolidation in 1897.

And so, brethren and friends, we come to the end of our journey, certifying that the men we have found in these pages are those that have matched our towering mountains of California, and that they will inspire each of us to deeds of continued exalted usefulness in the future we share together.

Order from:
Neyenesch Printers, Inc.
2750 Kettner Blvd.
P. O. Box 430
San Diego, Calif. 92112

Price $3.15 tax inc.
Hard covers $5.20 tax inc.
Additional copies available